THE COM

SousVide
SUPREME
COOKBOOK

Easy, delicious, state-of-the-art cooking

Jo McAuley

hamlyn

An Hachette UK Company
www.hachette.co.uk

First published in Great Britain in 2016 by Hamlyn,
a division of Octopus Publishing Group Ltd
Carmelite House
50 Victoria Embankment
London EC4Y 0DZ
www.octopusbooks.co.uk

ISBN 978-0-600-63271-9

A CIP catalogue record for this book is available
from the British Library

Printed and bound in China

10 9 8 7 6 5 4 3 2 1

Both imperial and metric measurements have been given in all
recipes. Use one set of measurements only and not a mixture
of both.

The cooking pouches used have an approximate capacity of
1 litre (1 quart) for the small and 4 litres (1 gallon) for the
large and measure 20 × 30 cm (8 × 12 inch) and 28 × 40 cm
(11 × 16 inch) respectively.

Standard level spoon measurements are used in all recipes:
1 tablespoon = one 15 ml spoon; 1 teaspoon = one 5 ml spoon.

Eggs should be medium, milk should be full fat, pepper should
be freshly ground and fresh herbs should be used unless
otherwise stated.

This book includes dishes made with nuts and nut derivatives.
It is advisable for those with known allergic reactions to
nuts and nut derivatives and those who may be potentially
vulnerable to these allergies, to avoid dishes made with nuts
and nut oils. It is also prudent to check the labels of pre-
prepared ingredients for the inclusion of nut derivatives.

Individuals who are immuno-compromised for any reason
should not eat rare or raw food; they should only eat food
cooked at or above 60°C (140°F) for a sufficient amount
of time to ensure the food is pasteurized.

Contents

Introduction

What is 'sous vide'?

Sous vide (pronounced 'sue veed') is a French term which is literally translated as 'under vacuum'. It has become the latest cooking technique to take enthusiastic home cooks by storm. Until recently, it was a cooking process that remained a well-kept secret among chefs around the world. Since the technology has become more affordable, it is now possible to find well-built, easy-to-use, high-quality sous vide water ovens suitable for any kitchen, resulting in an accessible form of cooking for chefs and home cooks alike.

The sous vide technique involves food being vacuum-sealed in special food-grade cooking pouches, which are then submerged in a water oven. The water oven is controlled to extremely precise temperatures, preventing food becoming overcooked, to deliver consistently perfect results.

What are the benefits of sous vide?

Less time spent in the kitchen – This technique reduces the hands-on cooking time necessary with most other methods. There are no special skills to master either – just submerge your packaged food and let your water oven do the work!

No guess, less stress – There is no need to worry about ruining that expensive cut of meat or piece of fish because, by following some very simple cooking times and temperature guidelines (*see pages 8–9*), it is virtually impossible to overcook your food. Controlling the cooking temperatures to an extremely precise degree means that your food will be cooked perfectly from edge to edge, resulting in texture that is impossible to achieve with other forms of cooking. This is particularly impressive when using cheaper and tougher meat cuts. Cooking such cuts of meat at a precise temperature over a long period of time will break down fat and connective tissue, resulting in incredibly tasty meat with the texture of fillet steak.

Locked-in goodness – Due to your food being vacuum-sealed in pouches, the nutritional benefits remain higher than conventional forms of cooking. Rather than being allowed to evaporate through steam or escape into boiling water the nutrients present in your food are retained in the cooking pouch. There is also no need to add fat or oil to the food in order to keep it moist, as the natural juices will do this for you. The health benefits are obvious.

A compact water oven is perfect for the home cook.

Full of flavour – As with the nutrients in your food, the flavour has no means of escape. All of the juices and aromas in the pouch continue to penetrate and infuse themselves into the food during the cooking process, resulting in wonderful tastiness.

No more ruined meals due to late dinner guests – Because food is held in the oven at such a precise temperature, it will stay at the same level of 'doneness'. For example, if you want to cook a medium rare steak, you just need to set your oven to the correct temperature and leave it for the minimum cooking time (*see page 8*). Once that time has been reached, your steak will remain at the same temperature all the way through for several hours.

Economical form of cooking – Not only does a water oven consume very little electricity, even over prolonged cooking periods, it is also possible to cook in bulk. Buy pieces of meat when they are on offer and then cook them in individual pouches at the same time. Quick-chill (*see page 7*) and freeze for future use so that you always have cooked food available when you need it. Cheaper cuts of meat cooked slowly in your water oven will result in incredibly tender pieces of meat with all the flavour locked in.

Preparation & cooking guidelines

The sous vide water oven is a surprisingly versatile piece of equipment and it is possible to cook all sorts of different foods with very good results. In addition to meat and fish, most fruit and vegetables cook beautifully using the sous vide technique, as well as eggs and egg-based dishes such as custard and ice cream base. You'll find lots of inspiration to tempt you within this recipe book!

Position your vacuum sealer with enough space to allow cooking pouches to lay flat while sealing.

A rack placed in the water oven is useful when cooking multiple pouches.

Water oven – Your water oven will come with its own set of manufacturer's instructions. Follow these to set up your oven correctly and familiarize yourself with its functions.

Vacuum sealer – Follow the manufacturer's instructions and familiarize yourself with the sealer's functions. Some vacuum sealers give the option of 'Normal' or 'Gentle' sealing speeds for 'Dry' or 'Moist' pouch contents. Where relevant, the recipes in this book have specified these settings.

Cooking pouches – Food-grade cooking pouches are available in a number of different sizes, as well as a roll that you cut to the desired size. If in doubt, go larger to ensure ingredients are comfortably packed. In this book, large and small pouches have been used and are specified where relevant.

Seasoning and serving – As a simple guideline to cooking individual foods such as a cut of meat, or a piece of fish, we recommend to season your food with whatever herbs and spices you desire and then seal in a food-grade cooking pouch. Season more lightly than usual as the flavour intensifies within the pouch. Once your food has been sealed it simply needs to be submerged in the water oven for at least the minimum length of time indicated in the cooking chart (*see pages 8–9*). However, most foods can then be left in the water oven for several more hours without altering the taste or texture. Once the pouch is removed from the oven you can either serve the food as it is or, alternatively, sear briefly in a very hot pan to create a golden crust.

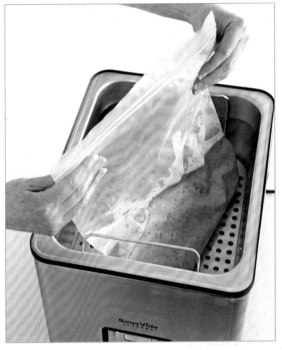

Archimedes principle, Step 1: removing air from and sealing the zip seal pouch.

Archimedes principle, Step 2: sealed zip seal pouch ready for submerging.

Archimedes principle – In the context of sous vide cooking, the 'Archimedes principle', otherwise known as the displacement method, is the term given to removing as much air as possible from a cooking pouch without the use of a vacuum pump. This is particularly useful when preparing liquid dishes. Place ingredients in a suitably sized zip seal pouch. With the zip seal open, slowly lower the pouch into the water oven until the water level reaches the zip seal – in so doing, as much air as possible will be forced out of the pouch by the pressure of the surrounding water. Zip the pouch firmly closed (Step 1), taking care not to allow any water from the oven to seep over the top and into the pouch. Once sealed (Step 2) the pouch must not float – this is a sign that too much air is in the pouch – but should remain fully submerged. Leave submerged for the indicated cooking time. **Do not attempt to seal a bag using this technique if the water in the oven is hot.**

Quick-chilling – Due to the lower than usual cooking temperatures, food which has been cooked according to the sous vide method should be eaten immediately. When this is not going to be the case then the food should be rapidly chilled and stored appropriately to be served at a later date. This process is referred to as 'quick-chilling'. To quick-chill your food, remove the pouches from the sous vide water oven and plunge directly into an ice water bath made up of half ice and half water. The pouches should then be fully submerged in the water bath for between 30 minutes and 2 hours, depending on the thickness of the food. If necessary, add extra ice to the ice water bath to keep the temperature below 5°C (41°F) throughout the process. Once the food has been chilled, the pouches (which have been appropriately labelled and dated) should be stored in the refrigerator for up to 48 hours, or alternatively should be transferred directly to the freezer.

Cooking temperatures and times – Follow these charts to obtain optimal cooking results when using your water oven. They provide the target temperatures and times required for foods according to the desired level of 'doneness'. Use these charts as a reference and adapt to your own personal preferences.

Doneness Target Temperatures

FOOD	DONENESS	TEMPERATURE	
		°F	°C
BEEF, VEAL, LAMB, GAME	Rare	120	49
	Medium rare	134	56.5
	Medium	140	60
	Medium well	150	65.5
	Well done	160 and over	71 and over
PORK	Medium rare	134	56.5
	Medium	140	60
	Well done	160 and over	71 and over
POULTRY, White Meat	Medium	140–146	60-63
DUCK, White Meat	Medium rare	134	56.5
POULTRY, Dark Meat	Well done	176	80
FISH, SEAFOOD	Rare	116	47
	Medium rare	126	52
	Medium	140	60
VEGETABLES, FRUITS	—	183–190	84-88
EGGS	Soft cooked	147 or 167	64 or 75
	Hard cooked	160	71
	Scrambled	167	75
	Pasteurized	135	57

Recommended Cooking Temperatures and Times

FOOD	THICKNESS[1]		TEMPERATURE		TIME	
	inch	cm	°F	°C	min	max
BEEF, VEAL, LAMB, GAME						
Tender cuts	1	2.5	134 or higher	56.5 or higher	1 hrs	4 hrs
Tenderloin, Rib-eye, T-bone, Chops, Cutlets	2	5	134 or higher	56.5 or higher	3 hrs	6 hrs
Tough cuts and Grass-fed [2]						
Bison, Game	1	2.5	134 or higher	56.5 or higher	8-10 hrs	12-24 hrs
Lamb roast or leg	2¾	7	134 or higher	56.5 or higher	10 hrs	24-48 hrs
Spare ribs	2	5	134 or higher	56.5 or higher	24 hrs	48-72 hrs
Flank steak, Brisket	1	2.5	134 or higher	56.5 or higher	8 hrs	24 hrs
	2	5	134 or higher	I56.5 or higher	12 hrs	30 hrs
PORK						
Tenderloin	1½	4	134 or higher	56.5 or higher	1½ hrs	6-8 hrs
Babyback ribs			165	74	4-8 hrs	24 hrs
Chops, Cutlets	1	2.5	134 or higher	56.5 or higher	2-4 hrs	6-8 hrs
	2	5	134 or higher	56.5 or higher	4-6 hrs	8-10 hrs
Roast	2¾	7	160-176	71-80	12 hrs	30 hrs
Spare ribs	2¾	7	160-176	71-80	12 hrs	30 hrs

FOOD	THICKNESS[1]		TEMPERATURE		TIME	
	inch	cm	°F	°C	min	max
Belly (quick)	2	5	185	85	5 hrs	8 hrs
Belly (slow)	2	5	167	75	24 hrs	48–72 hrs
POULTRY						
White Meat						
Chicken breast, bone in	2	5	146 or higher	63.5 or higher	2½ hrs	4–6 hrs
Chicken breast, boneless	1	2.5	146 or higher	63.5 or higher	1 hr	2–4 hrs
Turkey breast, bone in	2¾	7	146 or higher	63.5 or higher	4 hrs	6–8 hrs
Turkey breast, boneless	2	5	146 or higher	63.5 or higher	2½ hrs	4–6 hrs
Duck breast	1	2.5	134 or higher	56.5 or higher	1½ hrs	4–6 hrs
Dark Meat						
Chicken leg or thigh, bone in			165–176	74–80	4 hrs	6–8 hrs
Chicken thigh, boneless	1	2.5	165–176	74–80	2 hrs	4–6 hrs
Turkey leg or thigh			165–176	74–80	8 hrs	10 hrs
Duck leg			165–176	74–80	8 hrs	18 hrs
Game hen, split	2¾	7	150 or higher	65.5 or higher	6 hrs	8 hrs
SEAFOOD						
Fish	½–1	1.25–2.5	126 or higher	52 or higher	20 mins	30 mins
Tuna, Halibut, Snapper, Sole, Salmon, Trout, Mackerel	1–2	2.5–5	126 or higher	52 or higher	30 mins	40 mins
Crustaceans, Molluscs						
Lobster	1	2.5	140	60	45 mins	1 hr
Scallops	1	2.5	140	60	40 mins	1 hr
Prawns	jumbo	jumbo	140	60	30 mins	40 mins
VEGETABLES						
Root	up to 1	up to 2.5	183	84	1–2 hrs	4 hrs
Beetroot, Carrots, Celery, Parsnips, Potato, Turnips	1–2	2.5–5	183	84	2½ hrs	4 hrs
Tender	up to 1	up to 2.5	183	84	30 mins	1½ hrs
Asparagus, Aubergine, Broccoli, Cauliflower, Fennel, Green Beans, Onions, Peas (fresh), Squash, Sweetcorn						
FRUIT						
Firm	up to 1	up to 2.5	183	84	45 mins	2 hrs
Apple, Pear						
Soft	up to 1	up to 2.5	183	84	30 mins	1 hr
Apricot, Berries, Mango, Nectarine, Papaya, Peach, Plum						
EGGS[3]						
Soft-cooked in shell (quick)	large	large	167	75	15 mins	18 mins
Soft-cooked in shell (slow)	large	large	146	63.5	45 mins	1½ hrs
Hard-cooked in shell	large	large	160	71	45 mins	1½ hrs
Pasteurized in shell	large	large	135	57	1¼ hrs	2 hrs
Scrambled (5 eggs)	large	large	167	75	20 mins	2 hrs

[1] Thickness measurements are based on the thickest section of the food and measured through the vacuum-sealed pouch. Cooking times are for foods starting at refrigerator temperature. Add 15 minutes if starting from frozen.

[2] Tough cuts of meat will heat through to serving temperature in the same time as tender cuts. We recommend longer cooking times for lean, tough cuts to tenderize them.

[3] Eggs cooked in the shell should not be sealed in cooking pouches.

STARTERS & LIGHT BITES

Serves 4

Eggs Florentine with Asparagus Spears

4 large eggs

12 asparagus spears, trimmed

2 tablespoons butter, plus extra for buttering

150 g (5 oz) baby spinach

pinch of freshly grated nutmeg

200 g (7 oz) hollandaise sauce

2 muffins

Salt and pepper

◆ Fill and preheat the water oven to 63.5°C (146°F). Without using a cooking pouch, carefully place the eggs directly on the bottom grill of the water oven, so that they are completely submerged. Leave to cook for 1 hour 15 minutes.

◆ Blanch the asparagus spears in a pan of boiling water for 2–3 minutes, drain and keep warm.

◆ Melt the butter in a large frying pan, add the spinach and stir-fry for 3 minutes, or until just wilted. Season the spinach with grated nutmeg, salt and pepper.

◆ Heat the hollandaise sauce according to the packet instructions.

◆ Halve, toast and butter the muffins. Top each buttered muffin half with some wilted spinach.

◆ Remove the eggs from the water oven, pat dry and, one at a time, crack their shells and open directly on to the spinach-topped muffins. Repeat with the remaining eggs, then pour over the desired amount of warmed Hollandaise sauce. Sprinkle with pepper and serve each egg with 3 asparagus spears on the side.

Serves 4

Smoked Salmon & Scrambled Egg Bagels

2 x 150 g (5 oz) lightly smoked salmon fillets, 3 cm (1¼ inch) thickness
....

2 slices lemon
....

8 eggs
....

100 ml (3½ fl oz) milk
....

1 tablespoon chopped chives, plus extra to garnish
....

1 teaspoon chopped dill
....

25 g (1 oz) melted butter
....

4 bagels, split and toasted
....

125 g (4 oz) cream cheese (optional)
....

Salt and pepper
....

♦ Fill and preheat the water oven to 53.5°C (128°F).

♦ Lightly season the salmon fillets with salt and pepper and place each one into a small cooking pouch with a slice of lemon. Vacuum seal using the normal / dry setting of the sealer, then submerge in the water oven for 25 minutes. Remove and quick-chill the salmon (*see page* 7). Increase the temperature of the water oven to 75°C (167°F).

♦ Meanwhile, in a bowl, whisk together the eggs, milk, herbs and melted butter and season generously with salt and pepper.

♦ Divide the egg mixture between 2 small zip seal cooking pouches and remove as much air as possible using the Archimedes principle (*see page* 7). Seal and submerge in the water oven for 15–20 minutes, removing and gently massaging the pouch every 4–5 minutes until the eggs are cooked to the desired consistency.

♦ Return the salmon to the water oven for 5 minutes to warm, then remove from the pouches and flake gently.

♦ Spread the toasted bagels with cream cheese if using, and spoon over the scrambled eggs. Arrange the flaked salmon over the eggs. Serve immediately, garnished with chives and pepper.

Serves 4

Hot & Buttery Prawn Toasts

● Fill and preheat the water oven to 60°C (140°F).

● Place all of the ingredients except the bread in a large cooking pouch. Vacuum seal using the normal / moist setting of the sealer. Submerge for 40 minutes.

● Toast the bread for a few minutes, then pile the prawns and their juices over the hot toast.

● Garnish with chopped chives to serve.

450 g (14½ oz) raw prawns
....

100 g (3½ oz) cold butter, diced
....

Pinch of cayenne
....

1 tablespoon lemon juice
....

2 tablespoons chopped chives, plus extra to garnish
....

4 thick slices seeded bread, to serve
....

Serves 4

Moroccan-Style 'Baked' Eggs

3 tablespoons olive oil

1 onion, chopped

2 garlic cloves, chopped

1 teaspoon ras el hanout

½ teaspoon ground cinnamon

1 teaspoon ground coriander

2 x 400 g (13 oz) cans cherry tomatoes

1 small bunch of fresh coriander, chopped

4 large, free-range eggs

Salt and pepper

♦ Lightly grease 4 individual, ovenproof dishes with a little olive oil.

♦ Place a raised grill inside the sous vide water oven. Fill the oven with enough water to come about three-quarters of the way up the individual, ovenproof dishes once they are sitting on top of the grill. Preheat the water oven to 75°C (167°F).

♦ Heat the remaining olive oil in a heavy-based frying pan over a medium–low heat. Add the onion and garlic and cook for about 10 minutes, stirring occasionally, until softened and light golden in colour. Add the spices and cook for a further minute, then add the cans of cherry tomatoes. Season generously and simmer gently for 15 minutes until rich and thick.

♦ Stir 3 tablespoons of the chopped coriander into the tomatoes, then divide between the dishes. Crack an egg into each dish and cover tightly with clingfilm. Arrange on the prepared grill and leave to cook for 15 minutes until the whites have set but the yolks are still runny.

♦ Serve immediately, scattered with the remaining coriander.

Serves 4

Eggs 'en Cocotte' with Chives

Butter, for greasing

100 g (3½ oz) creamy blue cheese

150 ml (¼ pint) double cream

2 tablespoons chopped chives

4 large, free-range eggs

Salt and pepper

Buttered toast, to serve

♦ Generously butter 4 ramekin dishes.

♦ Place a raised grill inside the sous vide water oven. Fill the oven with enough water to come about three-quarters of the way up the ramekin dishes once they are sitting on the grill. Preheat the water oven to 75°C (167°F).

♦ Place the blue cheese in a small bowl with the double cream and mash together using the back of a fork. Stir in the chives, a little salt and plenty of pepper and divide between the 4 buttered ramekins.

♦ Crack an egg carefully into each ramekin, then cover tightly with clingfilm and arrange on the prepared baking grill in the water oven. Leave to cook for 20 minutes until the egg white is almost set but the yolks are still runny.

♦ Remove the ramekin dishes and slide under a preheated grill for about 1 minute until lightly golden. Remove and serve immediately with plenty of hot buttered toast.

Serves 4

Red Pepper, Butter Bean & Tomato Soup with Chorizo

2 x 400 g (13 oz) cans butter beans, rinsed and drained

1 red onion, chopped

2 garlic cloves, chopped

1 celery stick, diced

1 teaspoon whole cumin

200 g (7 oz) roasted red peppers

125 g (4 oz) sun-dried tomatoes, drained

400 g (13 oz) can Italian plum tomatoes

500 g (1 lb) passata

750 ml (1¼ pints) vegetable stock, plus extra if necessary

Salt and pepper

To serve

125 g (4 oz) diced chorizo

Fresh coriander, roughly chopped

♦ Fill and preheat the water oven to 88°C (190°F).

♦ Tip the beans into a large zip seal cooking pouch with all of the remaining ingredients and season with salt and pepper. Remove as much air as possible using the Archimedes principle (*see page* 7). Seal and submerge in the water oven for 1½ hours, or until the vegetables feel tender.

♦ Meanwhile, fry the diced chorizo in a small, dry frying pan over a medium heat until crisp and golden.

♦ Carefully remove the pouch from the water oven, then tip the contents into a saucepan and blend using a hand-held blender, adding more hot vegetable stock if necessary, in order to reach the desired consistency. Alternatively, blend in a food processor.

♦ Reheat slowly if necessary, then season to taste, ladle into bowls and serve, garnished with the fried chorizo and chopped coriander.

Tuna & Soba Noodle Salad with Ponzu Dressing

4 tuna steaks, about 125 g (4 oz) each, 2.5 cm (1 inch) thick

400 g (13 oz) dried soba noodles

½ cucumber, quartered and sliced

4 spring onions, sliced

4 tablespoons soy sauce

4 tablespoons mirin

Juice of 1 lime

1 tablespoon caster sugar

2 tablespoons vegetable oil

Salt and pepper

Sesame seeds, to serve

● Fill and preheat the water oven to 47°C (116°F).

● Season the tuna steaks with salt and pepper and divide between 2 small cooking pouches. Vacuum seal on the normal / dry setting of the sealer and submerge in the water oven for 20 minutes.

● Meanwhile, cook the noodles according to the packet instructions, then drain and cool under cold running water. Tip into a large bowl with the cucumber and spring onions.

● In a small dish, mix together the soy sauce, mirin, lime juice and sugar until the sugar has dissolved. Drizzle 2 tablespoons of the dressing over the noodles, toss gently to combine and divide between 4 serving bowls.

● Heat a griddle pan until smoking hot. Remove the tuna steaks from their pouches, pat dry with kitchen paper and then drizzle over the oil. Sear the tuna steaks in the griddle pan for about 30 seconds on each side until just lightly charred. Remove from the pan and cut into thin slices.

● Divide the tuna between the bowls of noodles, drizzle over the remaining dressing, then sprinkle with sesame seeds and serve immediately.

Serves 4

Peppered Tuna with Rocket & Parmesan

6 tablespoons olive oil

1 x 400 g (13 oz) tuna steak, about 2.5 cm (1 inch) thick

1 tablespoon mixed peppercorns, roughly crushed

1 tablespoon balsamic vinegar

100 g (3½ oz) wild rocket leaves

Salt and pepper

Parmesan cheese shavings, to serve

♦ Fill and preheat the water oven to 47°C (116°F).

♦ Brush the tuna steak with 1 tablespoon of the oil, then roll in the crushed peppercorns until well coated. Place in a small cooking pouch, vacuum seal on the normal / dry setting of the sealer and submerge in the water oven for 20 minutes.

♦ Whisk 3 tablespoons of the remaining oil with the vinegar until well combined, then season with salt.

♦ Heat the remaining 2 tablespoons of oil in a heavy-based frying pan. Remove the tuna from its pouch and sear for 30 seconds on each side until lightly golden. Place on a board and slice as thinly as desired.

♦ Toss the rocket with the dressing, season lightly and pile attractively on to serving plates with the sliced tuna. Sprinkle with Parmesan shavings and serve immediately.

Serves 4

Fennel, Ginger & Chilli-Spiked Mussels

75 g (3 oz) butter

....

1 small fennel bulb, finely chopped

....

2 banana shallots, thinly sliced

....

2.5 cm (1 inch) piece of fresh root ginger, peeled and finely chopped

....

2 garlic cloves, thinly sliced

....

1 red chilli, deseeded and finely chopped (optional)

....

50 ml (2 fl oz) Pernod

....

1.5 kg (3 lb) mussels, de-bearded and scrubbed

....

1 small bunch of fresh coriander, roughly chopped

....

♦ Fill and preheat the water oven to 93.5°C (200°F).

♦ Melt the butter in a frying pan and cook the fennel, shallots, ginger, garlic and chilli if using over a low heat for 8–10 minutes until softened and translucent but not coloured. Add the Pernod to the pan until evaporated and then remove from the heat.

♦ Divide the mussels between 4 large cooking pouches and then spoon the fennel mixture into each one with half of the chopped coriander. Vacuum seal on the gentle / moist setting of the sealer, then submerge for 15–20 minutes until the shells have opened.

♦ Discarding any that remain closed, heap the mussels and their cooking juices into deep bowls. Scatter over the remaining coriander and serve immediately.

Serves 4

Warm Chermoula Scallops with Green Beans & Watercress

20 king scallops, roes removed

375 g (12 oz) green beans, trimmed

150 g (5 oz) watercress and baby spinach leaves

Chermoula dressing

1 small bunch each of flat leaf parsley and fresh coriander, roughly chopped

½ teaspoon each of ground cumin, coriander, turmeric and ras el hanout

1 garlic clove, finely chopped

2 tablespoons lemon juice

3 tablespoons olive oil

Salt and pepper

⬦ Fill and preheat the water oven to 84.5°C (184°F).

⬦ Make the chermoula dressing by combining all of the ingredients in the small bowl of a food processor or a mini chopper and blending until smooth. Season with salt and pepper, then scrape half of the dressing into a large zip seal cooking pouch with the scallops. Massage the bag gently to coat, then refrigerate in the unsealed bag for 1–2 hours to marinate.

⬦ Meanwhile, place the green beans in a large cooking pouch, season with salt and pepper and vacuum seal on the normal / dry setting of the sealer. Submerge for 30 minutes, then remove and open the pouch and toss the green beans in half of the remaining dressing. Set aside and lower the temperature of the water oven to 60°C (140°F).

⬦ Remove the scallops from the refrigerator and, ensuring the scallops are arranged in an even layer, vacuum seal the pouch on the gentle / moist setting of the sealer, to avoid compressing the scallops too much. Alternatively, remove as much air as possible using the Archimedes principle (*see page 7*). Seal and submerge in the water oven for 40 minutes.

⬦ Toss the dressed beans briefly with the watercress and spinach leaves and pile on to serving plates. Remove the scallops from their pouch, arrange on the salads and serve immediately drizzled with the remaining dressing if liked.

Serves 4

Sweet Chilli & Coriander Salmon Fishcakes

500 g (1 lb) boneless, skinless salmon fillet, roughly diced
....

2 tablespoons sweet chilli sauce
....

1 large garlic clove
....

4 spring onions, finely chopped
....

1 small bunch of fresh coriander, finely chopped
....

2 kaffir lime leaves, finely chopped or 2 teaspoons finely grated lime rind
....

2 tablespoons vegetable oil, for frying
....

Egg fried rice or oriental-style salad, to serve
....

◆ Fill and preheat the water oven to 53.5°C (128°F).

◆ Place all of the ingredients except the rice in the bowl of a food processor and pulse quickly until chopped together but not a smooth paste. Alternatively, finely chop all the ingredients and mix together by hand.

◆ Scrape the salmon mixture into a bowl and use slightly damp hands to shape into 4 patties. Cover with clingfilm and place in the freezer for about 1 hour until almost firm. Alternatively, freeze completely and add 15 minutes to the cooking time.

◆ Divide the firmed patties between 2 small cooking pouches and vacuum seal on the gentle / dry setting of the vacuum sealer. Submerge for 20 minutes in the water oven. Remove and pat dry with kitchen paper.

◆ Heat the oil in a heavy-based frying pan until hot, then sear the fishcakes quickly for about 30 seconds on each side until slightly crisp and golden. Serve immediately with egg fried rice or an oriental-style salad.

Orange, Avocado & Chicken Salad with Walnuts

6 skinless chicken thighs

2 large oranges

2 small, ripe avocados

100 g (3½ oz) watercress

50 g (2 oz) walnut pieces

1 tablespoon walnut or olive oil

Salt and pepper

♦ Fill and preheat the water oven to 80°C (176°F).

♦ Season the chicken thighs with salt and pepper and place in a large cooking pouch. Vacuum seal on the normal / dry setting of the sealer and submerge for 4 hours. Remove and quick-chill (*see page* 7).

♦ Meanwhile, peel the oranges and cut into segments using a sharp knife, reserving any juices. Stone, peel and slice the avocados.

♦ Divide the watercress between 4 plates and arrange the orange segments and avocado slices attractively over the salad leaves.

♦ Remove the meat from the chicken thighs and shred over the salad. Scatter over the walnut pieces and serve drizzled with walnut oil and the reserved orange juice to your liking.

Fajita Chicken Sandwich

4 boneless, skinless chicken breasts, about 150 g (5 oz) each, 1.5 cm (¾ inch) thick

4 teaspoons fajita or similar Mexican-style seasoning mix

1 small red pepper, cored, quartered and deseeded

2 tablespoons olive oil

4 seeded soft bread rolls

1 ripe avocado, stoned, peeled and sliced

8 cherry tomatoes, halved

1 small red onion, peeled and thinly sliced

2 tablespoons chopped fresh coriander or flat leaf parsley

1 red chilli, deseeded and finely chopped (optional)

1 lime, quartered

Salt and pepper

Soured cream and chive dip, to serve

◆ Fill and preheat the water oven to 64°C (147°F).

◆ Season the chicken breasts with the fajita seasoning and divide between 2 small cooking pouches. Vacuum seal on the normal / dry setting of the sealer and submerge in the water oven for 1 hour.

◆ Meanwhile, arrange the peppers on a grill rack and place under a preheated grill for 8–10 minutes, turning occasionally, until lightly charred and slightly softened.

◆ Remove the chicken from the pouches and heat the olive oil in a large frying pan. Sear the chicken breasts for 30–60 seconds on each side until lightly golden.

◆ Arrange the chicken breasts in the bread rolls with the grilled peppers, the avocado slices, cherry tomatoes and red onion. Scatter over the chopped coriander and chopped red chilli if using and finish with a squeeze of lime juice. Serve immediately accompanied by the soured cream and chive dip.

Serves 4–6

Italian Bean Stew with Pancetta

3 tablespoons olive oil

300 g (10 oz) pancetta

1 onion, finely chopped

2 teaspoons chopped thyme

2 x 400 g (13 oz) cans borlotti beans, rinsed and drained

400 g (13 oz) can cannellini beans, rinsed and drained

200 ml (7 fl oz) vegetable or ham stock

Salt and pepper

Chopped parsley, to garnish

To serve

Crusty bread

Parmesan cheese

♦ Fill and preheat the water oven to 88˚C (190˚F).

♦ Heat the oil in a heavy-based frying pan and fry the pancetta over a medium high heat for 5–6 minutes until golden.

♦ Meanwhile, place all the remaining ingredients into a large zip seal cooking pouch. Add the cooked pancetta and a generous pinch of salt and pepper. Remove as much air as possible using the Archimedes principle (*see page* 7). Seal and submerge the pouch in the water oven for 1½ hours.

♦ Open the pouch, then divide the stew between warmed bowls and garnish with plenty of chopped parsley. Serve with crusty bread and freshly grated Parmesan cheese.

FISH & SEAFOOD

Serves 4

Creamy Prawn Korma

♦ Fill and preheat the water oven to 57°C (135°F).

♦ Reserve a large pinch of chopped coriander and then combine all of the ingredients except the rice in a large zip seal cooking pouch and season generously with salt and pepper. Remove as much air as possible using the Archimedes principle (*see page 7*). Seal and submerge in the water oven for 40 minutes.

♦ Open the pouch and pour the curried prawns into a warmed serving dish. Scatter the reserved coriander on top and serve at the table with plenty of steamed basmati rice.

50 g (2 oz) butter

1 small onion, finely chopped

2.5 cm (1 inch) piece of fresh root ginger, peeled and finely chopped

3 tablespoons korma or similar mild curry paste

400 ml (14 fl oz) coconut milk

Pinch saffron strands

50 g (2 oz) ground almonds

500 g (1 lb) raw peeled prawns

Small bunch of fresh coriander, chopped

Salt and pepper

Steamed basmati rice, to serve

Lemon Butter Fish with Herby Potato & Celeriac Mash

375 g (12 oz) peeled and diced celeriac

400 g (13 oz) peeled and diced floury potatoes

Pinch of grated nutmeg

4 thick white fish fillets such as cod, haddock or pollack, about 150 g (5 oz) each

Finely grated rind of 1 lemon

2 tablespoons chopped herbs such as parsley, chives, chervil and dill

50 g (2 oz) cold butter, cut into 4 slices

3–4 tablespoons crème fraiche, according to consistency desired

50 g (2 oz) melted butter

Salt and pepper

Steamed green beans, to serve

♦ Fill and preheat the water oven to 84°C (183°F).

♦ Combine the celeriac and potatoes in a large cooking pouch with the nutmeg and a generous seasoning of salt and pepper. Vacuum seal on the normal / dry setting of the sealer and submerge in the water oven for 1½ hours. Remove and reduce the temperature of the water oven to 55°C (131°F).

♦ Meanwhile, season the fish fillets with salt and pepper then scatter over the lemon rind and 1 tablespoon of the chopped herbs. Top each one with a slice of cold butter, then divide the fillets between 2 small cooking pouches, arranging them in a single layer. Vacuum seal the pouches on the gentle / dry setting of the sealer and submerge for 25 minutes.

♦ Tip the potatoes and celeriac into a food processor and purée until smooth, or pass through a mouli. Stir in the crème fraiche, melted butter and the remaining herbs, then season to taste and serve with the fish and its buttery juices and some freshly steamed green beans.

Serves 4

Griddle-Seared Hake with Chilli & Coriander Salsa

4 hake steaks, about 175 g (6 oz) each, 2.5 cm (1 inch) thick

4 tablespoons olive oil

2 green chillies, deseeded and finely chopped

2 red chillies, deseeded and finely chopped

4 cardamom seeds, ground

1 teaspoon caraway seeds, ground

1 garlic clove, crushed

25 g (1 oz) bunch of fresh coriander, finely chopped

1–2 tablespoons of lime juice, according to taste

Salt and pepper

To serve

Cucumber salad

Warmed pitta bread

◆ Fill and preheat the water oven to 55°C (131°F).

◆ Season the hake steaks with salt and pepper, then divide between 2 small cooking pouches and vacuum seal on the normal / dry setting of the sealer. Submerge for 20 minutes, then remove from the pouches and pat dry.

◆ Meanwhile, pour 3 tablespoons of oil into a small bowl and add all the remaining ingredients with a generous pinch of salt and pepper. Stir well to combine.

◆ Heat a griddle pan until hot. Drizzle the remaining oil over the fish steaks and sear the fish for 30–60 seconds on each side until lightly charred.

◆ Arrange the griddle-seared hake steaks on warmed serving plates and top each one with a spoonful of chilli and coriander salsa. Serve immediately with a cucumber salad and warmed pitta bread.

Red Mullet with a Summery Citrus & Radish Tabbouleh

375 g (12 oz) couscous

4 tablespoons olive oil

400 ml (14 fl oz) hot vegetable stock

2 oranges plus 4 orange slices

finely grated rind and juice of ½ lemon

4 red mullet fillets, about 150 g (5 oz) each

4 thyme sprigs

100 g (3½ oz) radishes, thinly sliced

75 g (3 oz) pitted black olives, chopped

handful of flat leaf parsley, chopped

Salt and pepper

♦ Fill and preheat the water oven to 52°C (126°F).

♦ Place the couscous in a large bowl with 1 tablespoon of the oil and stir well so that every grain is coated. Pour over the hot stock, cover and set aside for 10 minutes until all the liquid is absorbed and the couscous is tender.

♦ Add the finely grated rind and juice of 1 orange to the couscous with the lemon rind and juice and the remaining oil, then fluff with a fork and set aside to cool completely.

♦ Meanwhile, place the red mullet fillets in individual, small cooking pouches, each with a sprig of thyme and a slice of orange. Vacuum seal on the normal / dry setting of the sealer and submerge for 20 minutes.

♦ Peel the remaining orange, discarding any white pith, then cut into small pieces and stir into the couscous with the radishes, olives and parsley. Season to taste, then spoon into shallow bowls.

♦ Remove the red mullet from the pouches, discard the orange slices and serve with the tabbouleh salad.

Serves 4

Crunchy-Topped Red Pesto Cod

4 chunky cod fillets, about 150 g (5 oz) each, 3.5 cm (1½ inches) thick
....

25 g (1 oz) cold butter, sliced
....

4 lemon slices
....

75 g (3 oz) breadcrumbs
....

2 tablespoons red pesto
....

4 sun-dried tomatoes, finely chopped
....

Small handful of basil, chopped
....

1 tablespoon olive oil
....

Salt and pepper
....

Rocket, cherry tomato and olive salad, to serve (optional)
....

♦ Fill and preheat the water oven to 55°C (131°F).

♦ Season the cod fillets with salt and pepper, then top each one with a slice of cold butter and a slice of lemon. Arrange in a single layer in a large cooking pouch, then vacuum seal on the normal / dry setting of the sealer. Submerge for 25 minutes.

♦ Meanwhile, place the breadcrumbs in a bowl with the red pesto, sun-dried tomatoes and basil. Mix well to combine and season with salt and pepper.

♦ Remove the cod fillets from the pouch and carefully arrange on a baking tray, discarding the lemon slices. Top with the breadcrumb mixture and drizzle over the olive oil. Place under a preheated grill for 2–3 minutes until the breadcrumbs are just crisp and golden.

♦ Remove and serve with a rocket, cherry tomato and olive salad if liked.

Serves 4

French-Style Cod with Rich Tomato & Olive Sauce

4 chunky, skinless cod fillets, about 150 g
(5 oz) each, 3.5 cm (1½ inches) thick

4–5 small sprigs of thyme

2 tablespoons olive oil

1 onion, sliced

2 garlic cloves, finely chopped

1 tablespoon tomato purée

400 g (13 oz) can chopped tomatoes

pinch of sugar

25 g (1 oz) pitted black olives

Salt and pepper

new potatoes, to serve (optional)

♦ Fill and preheat the water oven to 55°C (131°F).

♦ Season the cod fillets with salt and pepper, then divide between 2 small cooking pouches. Add a small sprig of thyme to each pouch and vacuum seal on the normal / dry setting of the sealer. Submerge for 30 minutes.

♦ Meanwhile, heat the oil in a large high-sided frying pan. Add the onion and cook over a medium heat for 7–8 minutes until softened, then add the garlic and cook for a further 2 minutes. Stir in the tomato purée and cook for 1 minute, then pour over the chopped tomatoes.

♦ Strip the leaves from the remaining thyme and, reserving a few to garnish, add to the pan with the sugar and olives. Season with salt and pepper, then reduce the heat and leave to simmer, uncovered, for about 20 minutes, or until rich and thick.

♦ Remove the cod fillets from the cooking pouches and place gently in the sauce. Sprinkle over the extra thyme to garnish and serve with some boiled new potatoes if liked.

Serves 4

Plaice Fillets with Mussel & Cider Sauce

2 plaice fillets, about 200 g (7 oz) each, halved
....
50 g (2 oz) cold butter, diced
....
1 shallot, finely chopped
....
500 g (1 lb) cleaned live mussels
....
175 ml (6 fl oz) dry cider
....
4 tablespoons crème fraîche
....
Salt and pepper
....
handful of flat leaf parsley, chopped
....

◆ Fill and preheat the water oven to 60°C (140°F).

◆ Place the fish fillet halves in individual small cooking pouches with a pinch of salt and pepper and half of the butter. Vacuum seal on the normal / dry setting of the sealer and submerge for 30 minutes.

◆ Meanwhile, melt the remaining butter in a large saucepan and cook the shallot over a low heat for 6–8 minutes until softened.

◆ Increase the heat to medium-high, then pour in the mussels and cider and cook, covered, for about 5 minutes, or until the mussels have opened. Discard any that remain closed, then stir in the crème fraîche and season to taste.

◆ Remove the cooking pouches from the water oven and open. Place the plaice fillets on to warmed serving plates and spoon over the mussels and their sauce. Sprinkle with chopped parsley and serve immediately.

Serves 4

Salmon Steaks with Peachy Lime & Ginger Salsa

4 chunky salmon steaks, about 150 g
(5 oz), and at least 2.5 cm (1 inch) each
....

4 tablespoons olive oil
....

2 peaches, stoned and chopped
....

½ teaspoon finely grated fresh root ginger
....

juice of ½ lime
....

1 tablespoon finely chopped red onion
....

½ green chilli, sliced
....

handful of basil, chopped
....

Salt and pepper
....

♦ Fill and preheat the water oven to 55°C (131°F).

♦ Season the salmon steaks with salt and pepper and place in 2 small cooking pouches. Vacuum seal on the normal / dry setting of the sealer and submerge for 35 minutes.

♦ Meanwhile, mix 2 tablespoons of the oil with the remaining ingredients and season to taste. Set aside.

♦ Remove the salmon steaks from their pouches and pat dry with kitchen paper. Heat the remaining oil in a large, heavy-based frying pan and sear the steaks for 30–60 seconds on each side until golden.

♦ Arrange the salmon steaks on serving plates and spoon over the peach salsa to serve.

Herb-Crusted Salmon Fillets with Mascarpone

2 garlic cloves, crushed

1 teaspoon finely grated lemon rind

25 g (1 oz) parsley, finely chopped

1 small bunch of dill, leaves stripped and finely chopped

1 small bunch of tarragon, leaves stripped and finely chopped

4 tablespoons olive oil

4 chunky salmon fillets, 175 g (6 oz) each, about 3 cm (1¼ inch) thick

200 ml (7 fl oz) crème fraîche

125 g (4 oz) mascarpone

25 g (1 oz) unsalted butter

Salt and pepper

Steamed basmati and wild rice, to serve (optional)

♦ Fill and preheat the water oven to 53.5°C (128°F).

♦ In a bowl, combine the crushed garlic and lemon rind with half of the chopped herbs, 2 tablespoons of the olive oil and a generous pinch of salt and pepper. Add the salmon fillets to the bowl and turn to heavily coat in the mixture. Place each salmon fillet into a small cooking pouch, then vacuum seal on the gentle / dry setting of the sealer. Submerge in the water oven for 25 minutes.

♦ Meanwhile, combine the crème fraîche, mascarpone and remaining herbs in a bowl with a pinch of salt and pepper.

♦ Melt the butter with the remaining oil in a large, heavy-based frying pan over a medium–high heat. Carefully remove the salmon fillets from their pouches and sear for 30–60 seconds on each side until just golden. Lower the heat and spoon the mascarpone mixture into the pan, gently stirring around the fish until just hot, but not boiling. Remove from the heat and serve immediately with steamed basmati and wild rice if liked.

Whole Sea Bass with Spring Onion, Ginger & Soy

2 whole, gutted and scaled sea bass, about 375 g (12 oz) each

1 lemon grass stalk, cut in half lengthways

5 cm (2 inch) piece of fresh root ginger, cut into thin matchsticks

4 tablespoons Shaoxing wine

4 tablespoons soy sauce

3 tablespoons vegetable oil

2 teaspoons sesame oil

3 spring onions, sliced

Salt and pepper

steamed rice, to serve (optional)

◆ Fill and preheat the water oven to 52°C (126°F).

◆ Place the whole sea bass in a large zip seal cooking pouch with the lemon grass, half of the ginger and 1 tablespoon each of the Shaoxing wine, soy sauce and vegetable oil. Season with salt and pepper and ensure that the fish are laying flat in a single layer.

◆ Remove as much air as possible using the Archimedes principle (*see page* 7), or vacuum seal on the gentle / moist setting of the sealer. Submerge in the water oven for 25 minutes.

◆ Heat the remaining vegetable oil with the sesame oil in a small saucepan.

◆ Open the cooking pouch and carefully lay the fish on heatproof plates, discarding the lemon grass. Scatter the spring onions and remaining ginger over the fish and pour over the hot oil.

◆ Return the pan to the heat with the remaining rice wine and soy sauce and heat through briefly. Pour over the fish and serve immediately with steamed rice, if desired.

Swordfish Steaks with Homemade Pesto

4 swordfish steaks, about 150 g (5 oz) each, 1.5 cm (¾ inch) thickness

4 tablespoons olive oil

2 tablespoons lemon juice

Salt and pepper

Pesto

1 large bunch of basil, leaves removed

2 tablespoons lightly toasted pine nuts

1 small garlic clove, finely chopped

1 teaspoon finely grated lemon rind

125 ml (4 fl oz) olive oil

2 tablespoons freshly grated Parmesan cheese

Green salad, to serve

♦ Fill and preheat the water oven to 52°C (126°F).

♦ Place the swordfish steaks in a bowl with 2 tablespoons of the olive oil, the lemon juice and a generous seasoning of salt and pepper. Massage gently to coat, then divide between 2 small cooking pouches. Vacuum seal on the gentle / moist setting of the vacuum sealer.

♦ Refrigerate the swordfish for 30–60 minutes to marinate, then remove and submerge in the water oven for 20 minutes.

♦ Meanwhile, make the pesto. Place the basil, pine nuts, garlic and lemon rind in a food processor and blend until finely chopped. Stir in the oil and Parmesan and season to taste.

♦ Heat a ridged griddle pan until hot. Remove the pouches from the water oven, then open and pat the swordfish steaks dry with kitchen paper. Drizzle the remaining oil over the swordfish steaks and sear in the griddle pan for 30 seconds on each side until lightly golden. Serve immediately with the homemade pesto and green salad.

Parma-Topped Coley with Puy Lentils

4 thick coley fillets, about 150 g (5 oz) each

325 g (11 oz) dried Puy lentils

2 bay leaves

1 teaspoon salt flakes

4 slices Parma ham

5 tablespoons olive oil

2 tablespoons aged sherry vinegar

1 garlic clove, crushed

2 spring onions, chopped

100 g (3½ oz) baby spinach leaves

3 plum tomatoes, chopped

Salt and pepper

♦ Fill and preheat the water oven to 55°C (131°F).

♦ Season the coley fillets with salt and pepper and divide between 2 small cooking pouches. Vacuum seal on the normal / dry setting of the sealer and submerge for 25 minutes.

♦ Meanwhile, rinse the lentils, removing any debris, then drain, place in a large saucepan and cover with 3 times their volume of cold water. Bring to the boil, then reduce the heat to a gentle simmer. Add the bay leaves and salt flakes and simmer, uncovered, for about 20 minutes, or until just tender.

♦ Arrange the slices of Parma ham on a grill pan, then drizzle with 1 tablespoon of olive oil and place under a preheated grill for 2–3 minutes until lightly golden and slightly crispy. Remove and set aside. Mix the remaining oil with the vinegar and garlic.

♦ Cool the lentils slightly under cold running water, then drain well and remove the bay leaf. Toss through the spring onions, spinach and tomatoes, then stir through the dressing. Spoon on to serving plates.

♦ Remove the fish fillets from their pouches and arrange on top of the lentils. Top each one with a slice of crispy Parma ham and serve immediately.

Teriyaki-Glazed Tuna with Wasabi Mash

750 g (1½ lb) potatoes, peeled and quartered
....

4 very fresh, sushi-grade tuna steaks, about 150 g (5 oz) each, 2.5 cm (1 inch) thick
....

5 tablespoons soy sauce
....

2 tablespoons rice vinegar
....

2 tablespoons soft brown sugar
....

5 tablespoons crème fraîche
....

1 tablespoon wasabi paste
....

1 tablespoon vegetable oil
....

Salt and pepper
....

steamed sugar snap peas, to serve (optional)
....

◆ Fill and preheat the water oven to 84°C (183°F).

◆ Place the potatoes in a large cooking pouch with a generous seasoning of salt and pepper. Vacuum seal on the normal / dry setting of the sealer and submerge in the water oven for 1½ hours. Leave the potatoes in the oven to stay warm and reduce the temperature to 47°C (116°F).

◆ Season the tuna steaks with salt and pepper and divide between 2 small cooking pouches in a single layer. Vacuum seal on the normal / dry setting of the sealer and submerge in the water oven for 20 minutes.

◆ Meanwhile make the teriyaki glaze. Heat the soy sauce, vinegar and sugar in a small saucepan for about 2 minutes until the sugar has dissolved and the sauce is slightly syrupy.

◆ Mix the crème fraîche and wasabi together in a small bowl.

◆ Remove the pouch of potatoes from the water oven. Pass the potatoes through a potato ricer or mouli or mash until smooth. Stir through the wasabi and crème fraîche mixture and season to taste. Keep warm.

◆ Heat a ridged griddle pan until hot. Remove the tuna steaks from their cooking pouches, then pat dry with kitchen paper and drizzle with the oil. Sear for 30–60 seconds on each side until lightly charred.

◆ Spoon the wasabi mash on to warmed serving plates and top with the seared tuna. Drizzle over the warm teriyaki glaze and serve with some steamed sugar snap peas if liked.

Tuna Niçoise Salad

450 g (1 lb) tuna steak

2 eggs

300 g (10 oz) new potatoes, halved

100 g (3½ oz) green beans

2 Cos lettuces

125 g (4 oz) cherry tomatoes, halved

8 anchovy fillets in oil, drained

75 g (3 oz) black olives

1 tablespoon olive oil

Salt and pepper

For the vinaigrette:

1 garlic clove, crushed

1 teaspoon Dijon mustard

2 tablespoons red wine vinegar

6 tablespoons extra virgin olive oil

handful of parsley, chopped

◆ Fill and preheat the water oven to 52°C (126°F). Season the tuna with salt and pepper, then place in a small cooking pouch, vacuum seal on the normal / dry setting of the sealer and submerge for 20 minutes. Remove and quick-chill *(see page 7)*. Increase the water oven temperature to 71°C (160°F).

◆ Place the eggs in their shells directly on the water oven grill for 45 minutes, then remove and quick-chill. Increase the water oven temperature to 84.5°C (184°F).

◆ Place the potatoes into a large cooking pouch and the green beans into a small cooking pouch, season both and vacuum seal on the normal / dry setting of the sealer. Submerge both pouches, then remove the beans after 30 minutes, quick-chill and tip into a large bowl. Leave the potatoes submerged for a further hour, then remove, quick-chill and add to the bowl with the green beans.

◆ Mix all of the vinaigrette ingredients together and drizzle half over the potatoes and beans.

◆ Shell and quarter the eggs and arrange on serving plates with the lettuce leaves, potatoes and beans. Scatter over the tomatoes, anchovies and olives.

◆ Remove the tuna from its pouch, pat dry with kitchen paper and drizzle over the oil. Heat a griddle pan until hot and sear the tuna for 30 seconds on each side until just coloured. Cut into bite-sized pieces, scatter over the salads and serve with the remaining dressing.

'Chargrilled' Tuna Burgers with Sliced Mango Chilli Salsa

500 g (1 lb) piece of tuna, cut into large chunks

1 small shallot, finely chopped

1 tablespoon soy sauce

1 large mango, stoned, peeled and sliced

¼ red onion, thinly sliced

2 tablespoons olive oil

juice of ½ lime

½ red chilli, finely chopped

handful of fresh coriander, finely chopped

4 ciabatta rolls, split and toasted

Salt and pepper

⬧ Fill and preheat the water oven to 53.5°C (128°F).

⬧ Place the tuna in a food processor with the shallot and soy sauce. Briefly pulse until the mixture just comes together but isn't completely smooth. Alternatively, very finely chop and mix together by hand.

⬧ Using slightly damp hands, shape the mixture into 4 burgers. Cover with clingfilm and place in the freezer for about an hour until almost firm but not frozen. Alternatively, freeze completely and add 15 minutes to the cooking time.

⬧ Divide the firmed burgers between 2 small cooking pouches and vacuum seal on the gentle / dry setting of the sealer. Submerge for 20 minutes. Remove and pat dry with kitchen paper.

⬧ Meanwhile, toss together the mango, red onion, 1 tablespoon of the oil, lime juice, chilli and coriander. Season to taste and set aside.

⬧ Heat a griddle pan until smoking hot. Season the burgers with salt and pepper, then drizzle over the remaining oil and sear quickly for about 30 seconds on each side until nicely charred.

⬧ Serve the burgers on toasted ciabatta rolls with a spoonful of mango salsa inside.

POULTRY

Serves 4

Hoisin Chicken & Beansprout Pancakes

4 boneless, skinless chicken breasts, about 625 g (1¼ lb) total weight, cut into strips
....

1 tablespoon vegetable oil
....

4 tablespoons hoisin sauce, plus extra for dipping
....

1 teaspoon ginger paste
....

1 tablespoon dark soy sauce
....

150 g (5 oz) beansprouts
....

4 spring onions, cut into thin strips
....

½ cucumber, cut into thin strips
....

16 Chinese pancakes (the sort used for crispy duck), warmed
....

Salt and pepper
....

◆ Fill and preheat the water oven to 64°C (147°F).

◆ In a large bowl, combine the chicken strips with the vegetable oil, hoisin sauce, ginger paste, soy sauce and a pinch of salt and pepper. Mix really well to combine, then tip the mixture into a large zip seal cooking pouch.

◆ Ensuring the chicken strips are arranged in an even layer, remove as much air as possible using the Archimedes principle (*see page* 7), then seal and submerge for 45 minutes.

◆ Remove the chicken strips from their pouch, draining away any excess moisture. Divide the beansprouts, spring onions and cucumber among the pancakes, top with the chicken strips and roll up. Serve immediately with extra hoisin sauce for dipping.

Serves 4

Chicken & Bacon Caesar Salad

4 tablespoons olive oil

4 chicken breasts, skin on or off

½ ciabatta loaf, cubed

1 large Cos (or Romaine) lettuce, leaves separated

75 g (3 oz) cooked crispy bacon rashers, broken into pieces

6 tablespoons Caesar salad dressing

25 g (1 oz) Parmesan cheese shavings

Salt and pepper

◆ Fill and preheat the water oven to 65°C (149°F).

◆ Heat 2 tablespoons of oil in a large, heavy-based frying pan. Season the chicken breasts with salt and pepper and sear over a medium–high heat for 1–2 minutes on each side until golden. Remove from the pan, cool slightly, then divide between 2 small cooking pouches in a single layer. Vacuum seal on the normal / dry setting of the sealer and submerge for 1 hour.

◆ Meanwhile, place the ciabatta cubes on a foil-lined grill pan and drizzle over the remaining olive oil. Toast under a preheated medium grill for about 5 minutes, turning occasionally, until golden and crisp. Remove and set aside.

◆ Remove the chicken breasts from their pouches, pat dry with kitchen paper and cut into bite-sized pieces.

◆ Roughly tear the lettuce leaves and place in a salad bowl with the chicken and most of the bacon pieces. Add the toasted bread cubes and salad dressing and toss well to mix. Sprinkle over the reserved bacon pieces and the Parmesan shavings and serve immediately.

Italian Chicken Breasts with Red Pepper & Mozzarella

4 boneless, skinless chicken breasts, about 150 g (5 oz) each

1 tablespoon capers, rinsed and drained

150 g (5 oz) roasted red peppers

8 slices Italian salami Milano

125 g (4 oz) good quality mozzarella

2 tablespoons roughly chopped basil or flat leaf parsley

2 tablespoons olive oil

75 ml (3 fl oz) Italian dry white wine

Salt and pepper

Butter bean and rocket salad, to serve

◆ Fill and preheat the water oven to 65°C (149°F).

◆ Cut a chicken breast almost in half so that it opens into a 'butterfly' shape. Layer a quarter of the capers, peppers, salami and mozzarella over one side of the breast. Scatter over a quarter of the basil or parsley and season with salt and pepper. Fold the other side of the breast over the filling as tightly as possible. Repeat with the remaining chicken breasts.

◆ Place each breast into an individual small cooking pouch and vacuum seal on the gentle / moist setting of the sealer. Submerge for 2 hours.

◆ Heat the olive oil in a large, non-stick frying pan, then remove the chicken breasts from their pouches, reserving any cooking juices. Pat dry with kitchen paper and cook in the pan over a high heat for about 30 seconds on each side until golden. Remove the stuffed chicken from the pan and arrange on warmed serving plates.

◆ Deglaze the pan using the white wine and reserved cooking juices for 1–2 minutes until slightly reduced, then pour these juices over the chicken and serve immediately with a butter bean and rocket salad.

Serves 4

Thai Chicken Panang Curry

♦ Fill and preheat the water oven to 64°C (147°F).

♦ Place the cubed chicken breast in a large zip seal cooking pouch with all the remaining ingredients except the rice. Season with a pinch of salt and pepper. Remove as much air as possible using the Archimedes principle (*see page* 7), then seal and submerge for 1½ hours.

♦ Remove the chicken curry from the pouch and serve with steamed Thai jasmine rice, garnished with extra coriander.

625 g (1¼ lb) cubed chicken breast

1 bunch of spring onions, chopped

1 tablespoon freshly grated root ginger

1 lemon grass stalk, finely chopped

1 large bunch of fresh coriander, chopped, plus extra to garnish

2–3 kaffir lime leaves, finely chopped (optional)

50 g (2 oz) Thai Panang or Thai red curry paste

200 ml (7 fl oz) coconut milk

2 teaspoons Thai fish sauce

250 ml (9 fl oz) chicken stock

Salt and pepper

Steamed Thai jasmine rice, to serve

Serves 4

Greek Chicken Stifado

2 tablespoons olive oil

4 chicken legs, bone in

4 shallots, peeled and halved

1 large fennel bulb, trimmed and cut into wedges

400 g (13 oz) can artichoke hearts, drained and halved

100 g (3½ oz) kalamata olives

4 tablespoons sun-dried tomato paste

4 ripe tomatoes, roughly chopped

Small bunch of rosemary, leaves removed

500 ml (17 fl oz) hot chicken stock

Salt and pepper

Crusty bread or steamed basmati rice, to serve (optional)

◆ Fill and preheat the water oven to 80°C (176°F).

◆ Heat the oil in a large, heavy-based frying pan and place the chicken legs in the pan over a high heat for 3–4 minutes on each side until the skin is golden. Remove from the heat.

◆ Place all of the remaining ingredients in a large zip seal cooking pouch and add the chicken legs. Season with salt and pepper. Remove as much air as possible using the Archimedes principle (*see page* 7). Seal and submerge for 5 hours.

◆ Remove the pouch from the water oven, then ladle into warmed dishes and serve with crusty bread or steamed rice if liked.

Chicken & Apricot Tagine with Couscous

2 tablespoons vegetable oil

8 boneless, skinless chicken thighs, cut into chunks

1 large red onion, roughly chopped

1 cinnamon stick

1 teaspoon ground cumin

2 teaspoons ras el hanout

½ teaspoon ground ginger

1 teaspoon ground coriander

1 teaspoon paprika

175 g (6 oz) dried apricots

175 g (6 oz) dried prunes, roughly chopped

500 ml (17 fl oz) chicken stock

400 g (13 oz) can chickpeas, rinsed and drained

1 small bunch of fresh coriander, chopped

Salt and pepper

Steamed couscous, to serve

◆ Fill and preheat the water oven to 80°C (176°F).

◆ Meanwhile, prepare the tagine. Heat the oil in a large, heavy-based saucepan and cook the chicken in batches over a high heat, turning occasionally, until browned all over. Add the onion to the pan and cook for 2–3 minutes until lightly golden. Reduce the heat to medium and add all of the spices. Cook, stirring, for 2 minutes.

◆ Add the dried fruit, stock, chickpeas and half of the coriander, then tip everything into a large zip seal cooking pouch. Season with salt and pepper, then remove as much air as possible using the Archimedes principle (*see page 7*). Seal and submerge for 2 hours.

◆ Serve the tagine with steamed couscous and scattered with the remaining coriander.

Creamy Chicken, Chorizo & Broccoli Rigatoni

2 boneless, skinless chicken breasts, sliced

250 g (8 oz) rigatoni

125 g (4 oz) tenderstem broccoli spears

2 tablespoons olive oil

175 g (6 oz) chorizo, thickly sliced

200 ml (7 fl oz) crème fraîche

4 teaspoons chopped parsley

Salt and pepper

Freshly grated Parmesan cheese, to serve

◆ Fill and preheat the water oven to 65°C (149°F).

◆ Season the chicken with salt and pepper and arrange in a single layer in a small cooking pouch. Vacuum seal on the normal / dry setting of the sealer and submerge for 1 hour.

◆ Meanwhile, cook the rigatoni in lightly salted boiling water for 10 minutes, or until just tender, adding the broccoli for the final 5 minutes of the cooking time.

◆ Heat the oil in a frying pan, add the chorizo and stir-fry for 2–3 minutes, or until lightly golden. Stir in the crème fraîche, then remove the sliced chicken from the pouch and add to the pan with the chopped parsley. Stir through until hot, but not boiling, and toss through the pasta and broccoli.

◆ Season to taste then heap into warmed serving bowls and serve immediately with plenty of freshly grated Parmesan cheese.

Serves 4

Peppered Chicken with Goats' Cheese & Tomato & Basil Salsa

4 boneless chicken breasts, about 125 g (4 oz) each

2 ripe plum tomatoes, finely chopped

4 tablespoons chopped basil leaves

1 small red onion, finely chopped

4 tablespoons olive oil

1 tablespoon balsamic vinegar

4 thick slices of goats' cheese, rind removed

Salt and freshly cracked black pepper

To serve

Salad

Crusty bread

♦ Fill and preheat the water oven to 65°C (149°F).

♦ Cut the chicken breasts in half widthways, almost all the way through, opening the chicken out to form a 'butterfly' shape. Season all over with a little salt and plenty of freshly cracked black pepper and divide between 2 small cooking pouches. Vacuum seal on the normal / dry setting of the sealer and submerge for 45 minutes.

♦ Meanwhile, make a salsa. Mix together the plum tomatoes, basil, red onion, 2 tablespoons of olive oil and the balsamic vinegar. Season to taste with salt and pepper.

♦ Heat the remaining oil in a large, heavy-based frying pan. Remove the chicken breasts from their pouches and pat dry with kitchen paper. Sear over a high heat for 30–60 seconds on each side, or until golden. Place a slice of goats' cheese on top of each chicken breast and remove from the heat. Leave to rest for 2–3 minutes, or until the cheese is melting.

♦ Serve the hot chicken on warmed serving plates with the salsa spooned over and with a simple salad and crusty bread if liked.

Barbecued Poussins with Chilli Corn Salsa

finely grated rind and juice of 1 lime

2 tablespoons Cajun spice mix

3 tablespoons olive oil

2 poussins, each jointed in half and flattened slightly, 5 cm (2 inches) thick

175 g (6 oz) can sweetcorn

1 red chilli, finely chopped

¼ cucumber, finely chopped

Salt and pepper

⬥ Fill and preheat the water oven to 68.5°C (155°F).

⬥ Mix together the lime rind and juice, 1 tablespoon of the Cajun spice, 1½ tablespoons of the olive oil and a generous pinch of salt and pepper.

⬥ Place the halved poussins in a dish, pour over the spice mix and massage all over. Place each poussin half in a small cooking pouch and vacuum seal on the normal / moist setting of the sealer. Submerge for 6 hours.

⬥ Meanwhile, toss together the sweetcorn, chilli, cucumber and 1 tablespoon of olive oil.

⬥ Once the poussin halves are ready, remove from the pouches, sprinkle over the remaining Cajun seasoning and drizzle over the remaining oil. Arrange on a hot barbecue for 2–3 minutes, turning occasionally, until slightly blackened and the skin is crispy. Alternatively, place under a hot grill.

⬥ Serve the barbecued poussin pieces with the chilli corn salsa.

Serves 4

Crispy-Topped Turkey Parmigiana

4 turkey fillets, about 175 g (6 oz) each
....
1 tablespoon olive oil
....
2 garlic cloves, crushed
....
350 g (11½ oz) passata
....
1 teaspoon caster sugar
....
1 teaspoon dried oregano
....
75 g (3 oz) breadcrumbs
....
75 g (3 oz) freshly grated Parmesan cheese
....
150 g (5 oz) mozzarella cheese, sliced
....
Salt and pepper
....
Crusty bread, to serve (optional)
....

◆ Fill and preheat the water oven to 65°C (149°F).

◆ Season the turkey fillets with salt and pepper and divide between 2 small cooking pouches. Vacuum seal on the normal / dry setting of the sealer and submerge for 1½ hours.

◆ Meanwhile, heat the oil in a large, heavy-based frying pan over a medium heat and cook the garlic for a few seconds. Add the passata, sugar and oregano. Simmer for 5–8 minutes until thick and pulpy, then pour into a shallow, ovenproof gratin dish if the frying pan is not ovenproof.

◆ Remove the turkey fillets from their pouches and arrange on top of the tomato sauce.

◆ Mix the breadcrumbs with half of the Parmesan, then sprinkle over the turkey fillets. Scatter over the mozzarella and remaining Parmesan and place under a preheated grill for 2–3 minutes until the cheese has melted and the sauce is bubbling. Serve with crusty bread if liked.

Serves 4

Ginger & Coriander Turkey Burgers with Chilli Jam

450 g (14½ oz) minced turkey

1 teaspoon ground cumin

1 teaspoon ground coriander

½ teaspoon ground ginger

1 tablespoon freshly grated root ginger

1 garlic clove, crushed

3 tablespoons finely chopped fresh coriander

2 tablespoons vegetable oil

Salt and pepper

To serve

4 tablespoons chilli jam

4 toasted, Ciabatta-style bread rolls

Salad leaves

♦ Fill and preheat the water oven to 63.5°C (146°F).

♦ Place all the ingredients except the vegetable oil in a large bowl and season with salt and pepper. Mix thoroughly to combine, then form into 4 burger shapes. Wrap loosely in clingfilm and place in the freezer for 45–60 minutes, until firm, but not frozen. Alternatively, freeze completely and add 15 minutes to the cooking time.

♦ Divide between 2 small cooking pouches in a single layer, then vacuum seal on the normal / dry setting of the sealer and submerge for 1 hour.

♦ Heat a ridged griddle pan over a high heat. Remove the burgers from their pouches, then pat dry with kitchen paper and drizzle over the vegetable oil. Sear the burgers for about 1 minute on each side until a golden crust forms.

♦ Spread the chilli jam over 4 toasted, Ciabatta-style bread rolls, then top with salad leaves and the chargrilled burgers to serve.

Turkey, Mango & Coconut Curry with Poppadoms

1 tablespoon vegetable oil

1 large onion, chopped

1 teaspoon ground coriander

1 teaspoon ground cumin

2 tablespoons mild curry paste

500 g (1 lb) diced turkey breast

300 g (10 oz) fresh or frozen mango chunks

400 ml (14 fl oz) coconut milk

150 ml (¼ pint) rich chicken stock

6 tablespoons chopped fresh coriander

Salt and pepper

To serve

Crispy poppadoms

Steamed rice

♦ Fill and preheat the water oven to 64°C (147°F).

♦ Heat the oil in a large, heavy-based frying pan or wok and cook the onion over a high heat for 3–4 minutes until beginning to colour. Reduce the heat and add the spices and curry paste and stir for 1 minute. Remove from the heat.

♦ Place the diced turkey breast in a large zip seal cooking pouch and add the mango, coconut milk, stock and half of the chopped coriander. Scrape the spicy onion mixture into the pouch, massaging gently to combine. Season with salt and pepper, then remove as much air as possible using the Archimedes principle (*see page* 7). Seal and submerge for 2½ hours.

♦ Remove the pouch from the water oven and stir in the remaining chopped coriander. Ladle the curry into warmed serving bowls and serve with crispy poppadoms and steamed rice if liked.

Serves 4

Lemony Turkey & Broccoli Stir-Fry with Toasted Cashews

500 g (1 lb) skinless turkey breast, cut into strips

3 tablespoons vegetable oil

1 teaspoon lemon rind

2 tablespoons lemon juice

4 tablespoons light soy sauce

3 tablespoons clear honey

100 g (3 ½ oz) unsalted cashew nuts

250 g (8 oz) broccoli florets

1 large red pepper, deseeded and cut into pieces

3 spring onions, thickly sliced

2 tablespoons cornflour

200 ml (7 fl oz) cold water

Salt and pepper

◆ Fill and preheat the water oven to 64°C (147°F).

◆ In a large bowl, combine the turkey strips with 1 tablespoon of vegetable oil, the lemon rind, 1 tablespoon of lemon juice, 1 tablespoon of soy sauce, 1 tablespoon of honey and a pinch of salt and pepper. Mix well to combine, then tip the mixture into a large cooking pouch.

◆ Ensuring the turkey strips are arranged in a single, even layer, vacuum seal the pouch on the gentle / moist setting of the sealer. Submerge in the water oven for 45 minutes.

◆ Meanwhile, toast the cashew nuts in a small, dry frying pan over a medium–low heat for 3–4 minutes, shaking the pan occasionally, until golden. Tip into a small dish and set aside.

◆ Once the turkey has almost finished cooking, heat the remaining oil in a large wok or frying pan and cook the broccoli, red pepper and spring onions over a medium–high heat for 3–4 minutes until almost tender.

◆ Dissolve the cornflour in a small bowl with 1 tablespoon of the water. Stir in the remaining water, lemon juice, soy sauce and honey. Add to the vegetables along with the toasted cashew nuts and simmer, stirring, over a medium–low heat for 2–3 minutes until the sauce has thickened.

◆ Remove the turkey strips from their pouch, add to the pan and stir-fry for 1 minute until hot and bubbling. Serve immediately.

Chinese-Style Duck with Sugar Snap Peas & Orange Rice

2 tablespoons sesame oil

4 duck breasts, skin on, about 150 g (5 oz) each, 2.5 cm (1 inch) thick

2 teaspoons Chinese five spice

200 g (7 oz) easy-cook long-grain rice

finely pared rind and juice of 1 orange

2 tablespoons dark soy sauce

1 tablespoon soft light brown sugar

2 tablespoons vegetable oil

1 red onion, cut into slim wedges

1 bunch of spring onions, cut into 2.5 cm (1 inch) lengths

175 g (6 oz) sugar snap peas

Salt and pepper

◆ Fill and preheat the water oven to 65°C (149°F).

◆ Rub the sesame oil over the duck breasts, then season with the Chinese five spice and salt and pepper. Divide between 2 small cooking pouches and vacuum seal on the normal / moist setting of the sealer. Submerge for 2 hours.

◆ Meanwhile, bring a large saucepan of lightly salted water to the boil and cook the rice for about 15 minutes, or according to packet instructions, until just tender. Drain and keep warm.

◆ Mix together the orange rind and juice, soy sauce and sugar in a small bowl.

◆ Remove the duck breasts from their pouches, pat dry with kitchen paper and slice thickly.

◆ Heat the vegetable oil in a large wok or heavy-based frying pan over a medium–high heat and stir-fry the red onion for 5 minutes. Add the spring onions and sugar snap peas and stir-fry over a high heat for 1–2 minutes, until beginning to soften and colour slightly. Toss in the duck slices for 1 minute.

◆ Add the drained rice to the pan with the orange and soy mixture and toss quickly to combine. Serve immediately in warmed serving bowls.

MEAT

Garlic & Sage Marinated Pork Fillet with Wilted Spinach

2 garlic cloves, crushed

2 tablespoons chopped sage

Finely grated rind and juice of 1 lemon

4 tablespoons olive oil

1 whole pork fillet, about 500 g (1 lb) total weight, cut into 4 steaks

2 teaspoons clear honey

3 shallots, thinly sliced

300 g (10 oz) baby leaf spinach

Salt and pepper

Caperberries, to garnish

♦ Place the garlic, sage, lemon rind and 2 tablespoons of the olive oil in a mini chopper or pestle and mortar then blend or grind to make a rough paste. Scrape into a large cooking pouch with the pork fillets, honey and a generous pinch of salt and pepper. Massage well to coat and ensure the pork fillet steaks are arranged in a single layer. Vacuum seal on the gentle / moist setting of the sealer and refrigerate overnight to marinate.

♦ Fill and preheat the water oven to 57.5°C (135°F) and submerge the pouch for 2½ hours.

♦ Heat the remaining oil in a large frying pan, remove the pork fillet steaks from their pouch and sear over a high heat for 30–60 seconds on each side until lightly golden. Remove and keep warm.

♦ Add the sliced shallots to the pan and cook over a medium–low heat for 5–6 minutes until softened and lightly golden. Add the spinach to the pan with a generous pinch of salt and pepper and stir until wilted. Squeeze over the lemon juice, then spoon onto warmed serving plates. Top each plate of spinach with a pork fillet steak and drizzle over any juices. Serve immediately, garnished with caperberries.

Toulouse Sausage & Bean Hotpot

1 tablespoon olive oil

8 Toulouse sausages

1 red onion, sliced

2 Romero red peppers, cored, deseeded and cut into chunks

1 tablespoon rosemary leaves

400 g (13 oz) can adzuki beans (or any other canned pulse), drained and rinsed

400 g (13 oz) can butter beans, drained and rinsed

400 g (13 oz) can cherry tomatoes

1 tablespoon tomato purée

150 ml (¼ pint) beef or vegetable stock

Warm crusty bread, to serve (optional)

♦ Fill and preheat the water oven to 60°C (140°F).

♦ Heat the oil in a large, heavy-based frying pan and cook the sausages over a high heat, turning frequently, for 3–4 minutes until browned all over. Remove with a slotted spoon, then add the onion and red peppers to the pan and fry for 2–3 minutes until lightly golden. Remove the pan from the heat.

♦ Place all of the remaining ingredients into a large zip seal cooking pouch with the browned sausages, onions and peppers. Remove as much air as possible using the Archimedes principle (*see page* 7). Seal and submerge for 2 hours.

♦ Ladle into warmed serving bowls and serve with warm crusty bread if liked.

Serves 4

Honey-Glazed Pork Chops with Spinach Mash

750 g (1½ lb) potatoes, peeled and quartered
....

4 thick pork chops, about 2.5 cm (1 inch) thick
....

4 sprigs of thyme
....

3 tablespoons crème fraîche
....

50 g (2 oz) butter
....

200 g (7 oz) spinach leaves
....

1 tablespoon clear honey
....

1 tablespoon wholegrain mustard
....

Salt and pepper
....

♦ Fill and preheat the water oven to 84°C (183°F).

♦ Place the potatoes in a large cooking pouch with a generous seasoning of salt and pepper. Vacuum seal on the normal / dry setting of the sealer and submerge for about 1½ hours, or until the potatoes are tender. Leaving the potatoes in the water bath, reduce the temperature to 60°C (140°F).

♦ Season the pork chops with salt and pepper and arrange in a single layer in a large cooking pouch with the sprigs of thyme. Vacuum seal on the normal / dry setting of the sealer and submerge for 3 hours.

♦ Once the pork has almost reached its desired cooking time, remove the pouch of potatoes from the water oven. Pass the potatoes through a potato ricer or mouli or mash until smooth. Stir through the crème fraîche and season to taste.

♦ Melt the butter in a large saucepan and cook the spinach over a medium heat, stirring, for 2 minutes until just wilted, then stir it into the mash. Keep warm.

♦ Remove the pork chops from their cooking pouch and pat dry with kitchen paper, discarding the thyme. Mix together the honey and mustard, then brush over the chops. Arrange on a foil-lined grill rack and place under a hot grill for 2–3 minutes, turning once, until the glaze is bubbling and golden.

♦ Spoon the potato and spinach mash onto warmed plates and serve with the honey-glazed pork.

Fruity Stuffed Pork Fillet with Rosemary

2 pork fillets, about 250–300 g (8–10 oz) each

3 tablespoons roughly chopped rosemary leaves

4 tablespoons olive oil

1 onion, finely chopped

2 fresh peaches, stoned and roughly chopped

½ teaspoon ground coriander

Pinch of ground cumin

Salt and pepper

♦ Fill and preheat the water oven to 60°C (140°F).

♦ Lay the pork fillets on a chopping board and make a cut across the meat lengthways through the centre, about 1.5 cm (¾ inch) away from the other side (do not cut all the way through), and open out. Scatter the rosemary leaves over both the inside and outside of the meat pieces and season generously with pepper.

♦ Heat 2 tablespoons of the oil in a large frying pan and cook the onion over a medium–low heat, stirring, for 7–8 minutes until softened. Add the peaches and spices and cook for 1 minute.

♦ Spoon half the peach mixture down the centre of one of the fillets and the remaining mixture down the centre of the other. Gently press the meat back together and tie with kitchen string in several places to hold the stuffing in place.

♦ Season the surface of the pork with salt and pepper and then transfer to a large cooking pouch. Vacuum seal on the gentle / dry setting of the sealer so as not to deform the shape of the tied pork, then submerge for 2 hours.

♦ Remove the pork from its cooking pouch and pat dry with kitchen paper. Heat the remaining oil in the cleaned frying pan and sear the pork over a high heat, turning frequently, for 2–3 minutes until golden all over. Serve immediately, sliced into rounds.

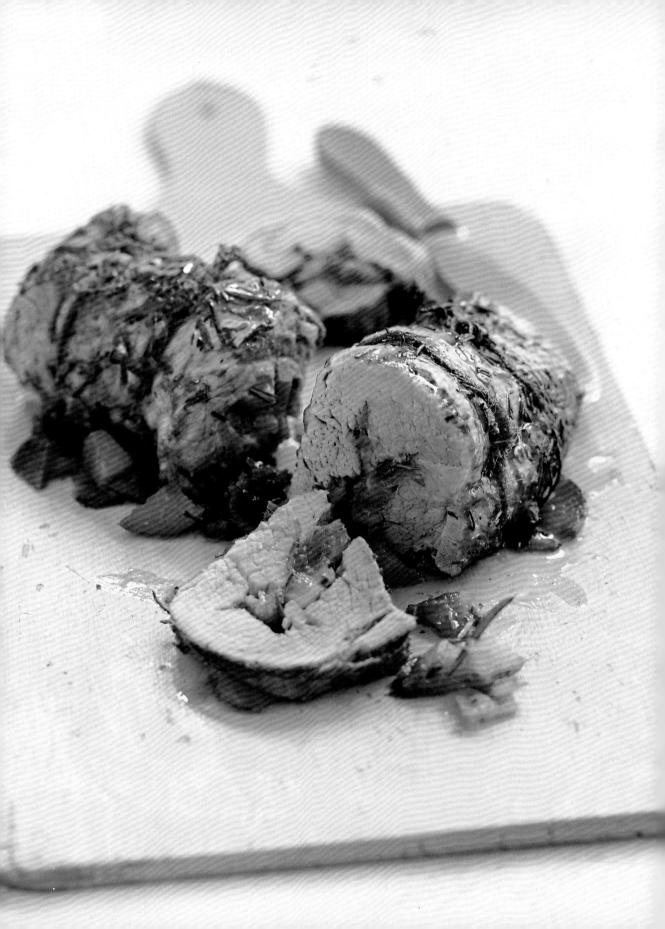

Serves 4

Sticky Southern-Style BBQ Ribs

4 racks short pork ribs, about 300 g (10 oz) each
....

125 g (4 oz) tomato ketchup
....

75 g (3 oz) dark brown sugar
....

4 tablespoons clear honey
....

3 tablespoons dark soy sauce
....

1 tablespoon Worcestershire sauce
....

Corn salad
....

2 x 200 g (7 oz) cans sweetcorn, drained
....

2 red peppers, deseeded and sliced
....

8 spring onions, finely chopped
....

1 large bunch flat leaf parsley, chopped
....

3 tablespoons olive oil
....

2 tablespoons lime juice
....

Salt and pepper
....

♦ Fill and preheat the water oven to 75°C (167°F).

♦ Score the pork between each rib bone with a sharp knife so that the marinade will be able to penetrate between the ribs.

♦ In a large bowl, combine the tomato ketchup, sugar, honey, soy sauce and Worcestershire sauce. Season with salt and pepper, then add the ribs and mix really well to coat in the marinade. Place each rack of ribs into its own large cooking pouch and vacuum seal on the normal / moist setting of the sealer. Submerge for 18 hours.

♦ Meanwhile, combine all the ingredients for the corn salad in a bowl and season to taste.

♦ Remove the ribs from the pouches and place on a preheated barbecue or under a preheated grill for 2–3 minutes until slightly blackened. Carefully cut the racks into individual ribs and serve with the corn salad.

Serves 4

Marinated Beef & Beetroot Salad with Blue Cheese Dressing

250 g (8 oz) small beetroot, stalks removed and peeled

3 tablespoons olive oil

2 tablespoons balsamic vinegar

2 teaspoons clear honey

400 g (13 oz) rump or sirloin steak, about 2.5 cm (1 inch) thick

Finely grated rind of 1 lemon and 1½ tablespoons juice

2 tablespoons chopped chives

75 g (3 oz) creamy blue cheese such as Gorgonzola or Roquefort

100 ml (3½ fl oz) soured cream

125 g (4 oz) bistro-style salad leaves

175 g (6 oz) runner beans, thinly sliced

Small bunch of radishes, finely sliced

75 g (3 oz) walnut pieces

Salt and pepper

◆ Fill and preheat the water oven to 84°C (183°F).

◆ Place the beetroot in a large zip seal cooking pouch with 1 tablespoon of the oil, the balsamic vinegar, honey and a pinch of salt and pepper. Vacuum seal in an even layer on the gentle / moist setting of the sealer. Alternatively, remove as much air as possible using the Archimedes principle (*see page* 7). Seal and submerge for 3 hours.

◆ Place the steak in a small cooking pouch with 1 tablespoon of the oil, the lemon rind and half the chives. Season and vacuum seal on the normal / moist setting of the sealer. Leaving the beetroot in the water oven, lower the temperature to 56.5°C (134°F) and submerge the steak for 1½ hours.

◆ Meanwhile, mash the blue cheese into the lemon juice, soured cream and remaining chives, then season to taste.

◆ Remove the beetroot from the pouch, then cut into wedges and arrange on serving plates with the salad leaves, beans, radishes and walnuts.

◆ Heat a ridged griddle pan until smoking hot. Remove the steak from its pouch, pat dry with kitchen paper and drizzle over the remaining oil. Sear for 30–60 seconds on each side until lightly charred. Slice thinly and arrange over each salad. Serve drizzled with the blue cheese dressing.

Serves 4

Cheesy Beef & Bacon Burgers

625 g (1¼ lb) good quality minced beef
....

125 g (4 oz) crumbled blue cheese such as Stilton
....

1 teaspoon dried oregano
....

8 smoked streaky bacon rashers
....

2 tablespoons vegetable oil
....

Salt and pepper
....

To serve
....

Large burger buns, cut side toasted
....

Salad leaves
....

Barbecue sauce
....

◆ Fill the water oven. According to taste, preheat to 56.5°C (134°F) for medium rare, 60°C (140°F) for medium or 65.5°C (150°F) for well done burgers.

◆ Place the minced beef in a bowl with a generous seasoning of salt and pepper, the crumbled blue cheese and dried oregano. Mix quickly and gently, taking care not to overwork the meat.

◆ Shape into 4 round burger shapes, about 2.5–3 cm (1–1¼ inch) thick, then divide between 2 small cooking pouches and vacuum seal using the gentle / dry setting of the sealer so as not to compress the burgers. Submerge in the water oven for 1 hour.

◆ Meanwhile, grill the bacon rashers until crisp.

◆ Heat the oil in a heavy-based frying pan, then remove the burgers from their pouches and pat dry with kitchen paper. Sear the burgers over a high heat for 30–60 seconds on each side until golden. Remove and arrange in a burger bun with fresh salad leaves, the crispy bacon and a generous helping of barbecue sauce.

Serves 4

Whole Fillet of Beef with a Mustard Crust

3 tablespoons vegetable oil

500 g (1 lb) whole fillet of beef

3 tablespoons wholegrain mustard

1 tablespoon Dijon mustard

3 tablespoons thyme leaves

2 tablespoons chopped parsley

For the wedges

4 baking potatoes, scrubbed and cut into wedges

2 tablespoons olive oil

½ teaspoon sea salt flakes

½ teaspoon English mustard powder

3 tablespoons chopped parsley

Salad leaves, to serve (optional)

♦ Fill and preheat the water oven to 56.5°C (134°F).

♦ Heat 2 tablespoons of the oil in a large, heavy-based frying pan and cook the beef briefly over a high heat, turning frequently, until browned all over and sealed. Transfer to a work surface.

♦ Mix the mustards and herbs together. Spread the mixture over the beef, then transfer to a large cooking pouch and vacuum seal on the gentle / moist setting of the sealer. Submerge for 2 hours.

♦ Meanwhile, spread the potato wedges out in a large roasting tin and drizzle with the olive oil. Toss well to lightly coat the potatoes in the oil, then scatter over the salt and mustard powder and toss again. Place in a preheated oven, 220°C (425°F), Gas Mark 7, for 20 minutes, or until tender and golden. Remove and scatter over the chopped parsley.

♦ Remove the beef from its pouch, then place on a foil-lined grill rack and drizzle over the remaining oil. Slide under a medium-hot grill for 2–3 minutes, turning frequently, until a thin crust has formed.

♦ Slice the beef into thick slices and serve with the potato wedges and accompanied by a simple salad if liked.

Serves 4

Rump Steak Bourguignon

4 rump steaks, about 2.5 cm (1 inch) thick
....
4 sprigs thyme
....
2 cloves garlic, sliced
....
4 tablespoons vegetable oil
....
200 g (7 oz) smoked bacon lardons
....
150 g (5 oz) portobellini or other small field mushrooms, sliced
....
200 ml (7 fl oz) Burgundy red wine
....
450 ml (¾ pint) good quality beef stock
....
50 g (2 oz) cold butter, diced
....
Salt and pepper
....
Mashed potato, to serve
....

♦ Fill and preheat the water oven to 56.5°C (134°F).

♦ Season the rump steaks with salt and pepper and place each one in a small cooking pouch with a sprig of thyme and a quarter of the sliced garlic. Vacuum seal each pouch on the normal / dry setting of the sealer and submerge for 1 hour.

♦ Meanwhile, heat 2 tablespoons of the oil in a frying pan and cook the bacon lardons over a medium-high heat for 2–3 minutes until golden. Add the mushrooms for a further 2–3 minutes until softened and golden. Pour in the wine and stir over a medium-low heat with a wooden spatula, scraping up any bits stuck to the base of the pan, until the wine becomes syrupy.

♦ Add the beef stock to the pan and simmer to reduce by half. Season to taste, then gradually whisk in the cold butter until the sauce is smooth and glossy. Keep warm.

♦ Remove the steaks from their pouches and pat dry with kitchen paper, discarding the thyme and garlic. Heat the remaining oil in a large, heavy-based frying pan and sear the steaks quickly on each side over a very high heat until nicely browned.

♦ Transfer the steaks to warmed serving plates and spoon over the Bourguignon-style sauce. Serve immediately with mounds of buttery mashed potato.

Smoked Salt Steak with French Bistro Salad

4 beef steaks, about 1.5 cm (¾ inch) thick

2 ripe tomatoes, diced

1 banana shallot, finely chopped

4 tablespoons olive oil

1 tablespoon wholegrain mustard

1 tablespoon red wine vinegar

400 g (13 oz) fine green beans, trimmed

200 g (7 oz) Bistro-style salad leaves

Smoked sea salt and pepper

Crusty French bread, to serve

◆ Fill the water oven. Set to 60°C (140°F) for medium steaks or refer to the 'doneness' guidelines on page 8 for other levels of cooking.

◆ Season the steaks with a pinch of smoked sea salt and pepper, then divide between 2 small cooking pouches in one layer and vacuum seal on the normal / dry setting of the sealer. Submerge for 2 hours (regardless of chosen 'doneness' temperature).

◆ Meanwhile place the diced tomatoes and shallot in a bowl with 2 tablespoons of the olive oil, the mustard and vinegar. Stir together and season to taste.

◆ Bring a saucepan of lightly salted water to the boil and cook the green beans for 2–3 minutes until just tender. Drain, return to the pan and add the tomato dressing. Toss gently to coat and set aside.

◆ When the steaks have finished cooking, heat the remaining oil in a large ridged griddle pan until smoking hot. Remove the steaks from their pouches, pat dry with kitchen paper and sear quickly for about 30 seconds on each side until just charred.

◆ Heap the dressed green beans on to a bed of Bistro-style salad leaves and top each one with a steak. Serve immediately with crusty French bread.

Serves 4

Creamy Coconut Beef Rendang

♦ Fill and preheat the water oven and set to 60°C (140°F).

♦ Pour the oil into a large, heavy-based frying pan and brown the beef in batches over a high heat, turning occasionally, until browned all over. Remove with a slotted spoon and repeat with the remaining meat.

♦ Place the browned beef into a large zip seal cooking pouch with the remaining ingredients and remove as much air as possible using the Archimedes principle (*see page* 7). Seal and submerge for 10–12 hours.

♦ Remove the beef rendang curry from its cooking pouch and serve immediately with steamed Thai jasmine rice scattered with chopped coriander.

2 tablespoons vegetable oil

750 g (1½ lb) diced braising steak

1 tablespoon peeled and finely chopped fresh root ginger

1 bird's eye chilli, thinly sliced

1 garlic clove, thinly sliced

1 lemon grass stalk, thinly sliced

1 small cinnamon stick

5 cardamom pods, lightly crushed

Finely grated rind and juice of 1 lime

1 tablespoon palm sugar or dark brown sugar

1 tablespoon tamarind paste

400 g (13 oz) can reduced fat coconut milk

4 tablespoons chopped fresh coriander, to garnish

Steamed Thai jasmine rice, to serve

Serves 4

Greek-Style Lamb with Spicy Tomato Salsa

1 teaspoon dried oregano

3 tablespoons olive oil

1 teaspoon grated lemon rind

4 lamb steaks, about 2.5 cm
(1 inch) thick

Salt and pepper

For the salsa

300 g (10 oz) ripe tomatoes, deseeded
and diced

½ red onion, finely chopped

1 large red chilli, deseeded and finely
chopped

Pinch of sugar

2 teaspoons lemon juice

1 tablespoon olive oil

2 tablespoons chopped flat leaf parsley

Steamed kale leaves, to serve

♦ Fill and preheat the water oven to 56.5°C (134°F).

♦ Combine the oregano, 1 tablespoon of the olive oil and the
lemon rind in a dish with a pinch of salt and pepper. Add the
lamb steaks, turn in the marinade until well coated, then transfer
to a large cooking pouch. Vacuum seal in a single layer on the
normal / moist setting of the sealer and submerge for 2 hours.

♦ Meanwhile, combine the salsa ingredients in a bowl and
season to taste.

♦ Remove the lamb steaks from their cooking pouch and
pat dry with kitchen paper. Heat the remaining oil in a large,
heavy-based frying pan and sear the steaks over a high heat for
30–60 seconds on each side.

♦ Serve each lamb steak on a mound of freshly steamed kale
leaves with a spoonful of the spicy tomato salsa.

Serves 4

Lamb Fillet with Madeira & Mushroom Sauce

2 thick end lamb neck fillet pieces, about 250 g (8 oz) each
....
3 tablespoons olive oil
....
4 thyme sprigs
....
2 sprigs rosemary
....
Salt and pepper
....

For the sauce
....
15 g (½ oz) butter
....
1 tablespoon olive oil
....
1 small onion, finely chopped
....
250 g (8 oz) chestnut mushrooms, trimmed and halved
....
100 g (3½ oz) button mushrooms, trimmed
....
½ teaspoon ground paprika
....
3 tablespoons Madeira
....
300 ml (½ pint) single cream
....
250 g (8 oz) spinach leaves
....

◊ Fill and preheat the water oven to 56.5°C (134°F).

◊ Season the lamb with plenty of salt and pepper. Heat 1 tablespoon of the oil in large, heavy-based frying pan and cook the lamb over a high heat, turning frequently, for 1–2 minutes until well browned and sealed all over. Transfer to a large cooking pouch with the thyme and rosemary and any cooking juices. Vacuum seal in an even layer on the gentle / moist setting of the sealer. Submerge for 24 hours.

◊ To make the sauce, melt the butter with the oil in a large, heavy-based frying pan and cook the onion over medium heat, stirring occasionally, for about 10 minutes until softened. Increase the heat slightly and cook the mushrooms for a further 5 minutes until soft and golden. Add the paprika and fry for 1 minute, then pour in the Madeira and cook for a few seconds until the alcohol has evaporated. Lower the heat, then add the cream and spinach and cook over a gentle heat, stirring occasionally, for 3–4 minutes until the spinach has wilted and the sauce is hot.

◊ Remove the lamb from its pouch and pat dry with kitchen paper, discarding the herbs. Heat the remaining oil in a frying pan over a high heat and sear the lamb quickly, on each side to form a crust. Remove and slice thickly then arrange on warmed serving plates and serve with the mushroom and spinach sauce.

Spicy Fruity Couscous

75 g (3 oz) sultanas

1 large preserved lemon, chopped

450 ml (¾ pint) hot lamb stock

4 lamb leg steaks, about 2.5 cm (1 inch) thick

350 g (11½ oz) couscous

1 tablespoon olive oil

Salt

Spicy yogurt paste

2 garlic cloves, crushed

2 tablespoons chopped mint, plus extra to garnish

1 teaspoon ground cumin

1 teaspoon ground coriander

¼ teaspoon ground ginger

1 tablespoon lemon juice

200 g (7 oz) natural yogurt

1 teaspoon harissa

1–2 tablespoons toasted flaked almonds, to garnish

♦ Fill and preheat the water oven to 56.5°C (134°F).

♦ Add the sultanas and preserved lemon to a pan with the hot lamb stock and set aside.

♦ Combine all of the ingredients for the spicy yogurt paste in a large bowl and add the lamb. Mix well until thoroughly coated, then scrape into a large cooking pouch in an even layer and vacuum seal on the gentle / moist setting of the sealer. Alternatively, use a zip seal pouch and remove as much air as possible using the Archimedes principle (*see page* 7). Seal and submerge for 2 hours.

♦ Mix the couscous in a large bowl with the olive oil and pinch of salt. Bring the fruity lamb stock to the boil and pour over the couscous. Cover and set aside for about 15 minutes until the couscous is tender and the liquid has been absorbed.

♦ Remove the lamb steaks from their pouches and arrange on a foil-lined grill rack. Slide under a hot grill for about 1 minute each side until just lightly coloured.

♦ Fluff the couscous with a fork, then spoon into serving dishes and top each one with a lamb steak. Scatter with the extra chopped mint and toasted almonds to serve.

Rosemary Lamb with Cannellini Mash & Roasted Cherry Tomatoes

8 lamb cutlets, about 2.5 cm (1 inch) thick

6 tablespoons olive oil

2 pinches smoked paprika

1 garlic clove, crushed

2 teaspoons finely chopped rosemary leaves

400 g (13 oz) cherry tomatoes on the vine

Salt and pepper

Cannellini mash

4 tablespoons olive oil

1 red chilli (optional), deseeded and halved

1 small sprig of rosemary

2 x 400 g (13 oz) cans cannellini beans, rinsed and drained

175 ml (6 fl oz) chicken or lamb stock

◆ Fill and preheat the water oven to 60°C (140°F).

◆ Place the lamb in a shallow dish with 2 tablespoons of the oil, the paprika, garlic and rosemary. Turn several times to coat. Transfer to a large cooking pouch in an even layer and seal on the normal / moist setting of the sealer. Submerge for 1½–2 hours.

◆ Arrange the cherry tomatoes in a small roasting tray and drizzle over 2 tablespoons of olive oil. Season with salt and pepper and roast in a preheated oven, 180°C (350°F), Gas Mark 4, for 15 minutes until beginning to collapse.

◆ Meanwhile, make the cannellini mash. Heat the oil in a large, heavy-based frying pan and warm the chilli and rosemary over a low heat for 3–4 minutes to infuse the oil. Remove the chilli and rosemary with a slotted spoon and discard.

◆ Add the beans to the pan for 1 minute, then pour in the stock and bring to the boil. Simmer gently for 4–5 minutes until reduced slightly. Mash with a potato masher or blend in a food processor until almost smooth but with some texture. Season to taste and keep warm.

◆ Remove the lamb cutlets from their pouches, then pat dry with kitchen paper and drizzle with the remaining olive oil. Sear the lamb cutlets in a hot, ridged griddle pan for 30–60 seconds on each side until lightly charred.

◆ Spoon the mash onto plates, top with the lamb and serve with the roasted tomatoes.

VEGETARIAN

Serves 4

Tunisian Chickpea & Vegetable Salad with Herby Harissa Dressing

3 large eggs

400 g (13 oz) can chickpeas, rinsed and drained

1 large red pepper, cut into large pieces

1 large green pepper, cut into large pieces

1 onion, cut into thin wedges

200 g (7 oz) button mushrooms

2 large green chillies, deseeded (optional) and roughly chopped

100 g (3½ oz) black olives, to serve

Lemon wedges, to serve

Harissa dressing

3 tablespoons chopped flat leaf parsley

3 tablespoons chopped fresh coriander

1 tablespoon olive oil

½ teaspoon ground cumin

½ teaspoon ground coriander

1 teaspoon of finely grated lemon rind

1–2 teaspoons good quality harissa paste (depending on heat required)

♦ Fill and preheat the water oven to 71°C (160°F) and submerge the eggs in their shells directly in the water oven for 60 minutes.

♦ To make the harissa dressing, place half of the parsley and fresh coriander in a large bowl with the remaining dressing ingredients and mix well to combine. Add the chickpeas and all of the vegetables except the olives to the dressing and toss to coat. Divide between 2 large cooking pouches, ensuring the vegetables are arranged in a single layer, and vacuum seal on the normal / moist setting of the sealer.

♦ Remove the eggs from the water oven, cool under cold running water and increase the water oven temperature to 84°C (183°F). Once the correct temperature is reached, submerge the pouches of vegetables for 20–25 minutes until almost tender.

♦ Shell and roughly chop the hard boiled eggs.

♦ Heap the warmed vegetables on to serving plates, then crumble over the hard boiled eggs and scatter over the black olives and the remaining herbs. Serve immediately with lemon wedges.

Hearty Mushroom & Tarragon Soup

625 g (1¼ lb) chestnut mushrooms, roughly chopped

4 shallots, chopped

1 trimmed leek, finely sliced

1 celery stick, chopped

2 garlic cloves, chopped

1 large potato, peeled and cut into 1 cm (½ inch) dice

1 tablespoon finely chopped tarragon, plus extra to garnish

75 g (3 oz) cold butter, diced

900 ml (1½ pints) vegetable stock

100 ml (3½ fl oz) single cream

Salt and pepper

Crusty bread, to serve

♦ Fill and preheat the water oven to 84°C (183°F).

♦ Reserving 100 g (3½ oz) of the mushrooms, place all of the remaining vegetables into a large cooking pouch with the tarragon and 50 g (2 oz) of the butter. Season with salt and pepper, then vacuum seal on the normal / dry setting of the sealer and submerge for 1½ hours.

♦ Meanwhile, melt the remaining butter and pan-fry the remaining mushrooms over a medium–high heat for 3–4 minutes, tossing occasionally until softened and golden. Remove from the heat and set aside to keep warm.

♦ Heat the vegetable stock to boiling point in a large saucepan.

♦ Remove the pouch from the water oven and tip the contents into the hot stock. Blend with a hand held stick blender until almost smooth. Stir in the cream, season to taste, then ladle into warmed bowls. Spoon the pan-fried mushrooms over the soup, then garnish with chopped tarragon and serve with plenty of warm, crusty bread.

Serves 4

Moroccan-Style Tomato, Pepper & Chickpea Stew

♦ Fill and preheat the water oven to 84°C (183°F).

♦ Place all of the ingredients into a large zip seal cooking pouch. Season with salt and pepper and massage the bag to mix the contents. Remove as much air as possible using the Archimedes principle (*see page 7*). Seal and submerge for 1½ hours.

♦ Remove the pouch from the water oven, then ladle the stew into warmed bowls and scatter with chopped parsley to serve.

1 large onion, chopped

1 green pepper, deseeded and roughly chopped

1 garlic clove, chopped

2.5 cm (1 inch) piece of ginger, peeled and chopped

1 teaspoon cumin seeds

1 teaspoon ras el hanout

2 tablespoons tomato purée

400 ml (14 fl oz) vegetable stock

4 tomatoes, quartered

2 x 400 g (13 oz) cans chickpeas, rinsed and drained

Salt and pepper

Chopped flat leaf parsley, to garnish

Serves 4

Creamy Goats' Cheese & Spinach Risotto

50 g (2 oz) butter

1 large onion, thinly sliced

1 garlic clove, chopped

250 g (8 oz) Arborio risotto rice

125 ml (4 fl oz) dry white wine

750 ml (1¼ pints) hot vegetable stock

1 tablespoon olive oil

300 g (10 oz) spinach leaves

Finely grated rind and juice of 1 lemon

175 g (6 oz) goats' cheese, roughly chopped into cubes

Salt and pepper

Freshly grated Parmesan cheese, to serve

◆ Fill and preheat the water oven to 83.5°C (182°F).

◆ Melt the butter in a large, heavy-based frying pan and cook the onion and garlic over a medium–low heat, stirring occasionally, for 5–6 minutes until softened.

◆ Add the rice and cook, stirring, for 1 minute, then pour in the wine and stir until absorbed.

◆ Scrape into a large zip seal cooking pouch with the stock and a generous seasoning of salt and pepper, then remove as much air as possible using the Archimedes principle (see page 7). Seal and submerge for 45–50 minutes, massaging occasionally, until the rice is just tender and the liquid has been absorbed.

◆ Meanwhile, heat the olive oil in a large pan, add the spinach leaves, lemon rind and juice and cook, stirring, for 2–3 minutes until the spinach has wilted.

◆ Remove the cooking pouch from the water oven, then tip the contents into the pan and stir gently into the spinach. Season to taste.

◆ Scatter the goats' cheese over the risotto until just beginning to melt, then spoon into warmed serving bowls. Sprinkle over the grated Parmesan cheese and serve immediately.

Butternut Squash & Courgette Tagine

♦ Fill and preheat the water oven to 84°C (183°F).

♦ Place all of the ingredients in a large zip seal cooking pouch and season generously. Remove as much air as possible using the Archimedes principle (*see page* 7), then seal and submerge for 1½ hours.

♦ Remove the pouch from the water oven and transfer the tagine to a warmed serving dish. Scatter with chopped coriander and flaked almonds and serve.

500 g (1 lb) peeled butternut squash, cut into chunks

1 red onion, cut into wedges

2 garlic cloves, chopped

1.5 cm (¾ inch) piece root ginger, chopped

2 teaspoons ras el hanout

Pinch saffron strands (optional)

1 courgette, cut into chunks

400 g (13 oz) can chickpeas

400 g (13 oz) can chopped tomatoes

2 teaspoons clear honey

125 ml (4 fl oz) vegetable stock

Salt and pepper

To garnish

Chopped fresh coriander

Toasted flaked almonds

Serves 4

Cheesy Sweet Potato & Tomato Gratin with Caramelized Onions

75 g (3 oz) butter

2 red onions, sliced

750 g (1½ lb) sweet potatoes, peeled and thickly sliced

3 tomatoes, thickly sliced

2 tablespoons chopped flat leaf parsley

25 g (1 oz) plain flour

300 ml (½ pint) milk

½ teaspoon freshly grated nutmeg

1 teaspoon Dijon mustard

150 g (5 oz) Emmental or Gruyère cheese, grated

Salt and pepper

Green salad, to serve

◆ Fill and preheat the water oven to 84°C (183°F).

◆ Melt 50 g (2 oz) of the butter in a large, heavy-based frying pan and cook the onions over a medium–low heat, stirring occasionally, for 10–15 minutes until soft and golden.

◆ Place the sweet potato slices in a large cooking pouch with the caramelized onions, tomatoes and chopped parsley. Season generously with salt and pepper, arrange in an even layer and vacuum seal on the normal / dry setting of the sealer. Submerge for 1 hour.

◆ Meanwhile, melt the remaining butter in a saucepan, add the flour and cook over a medium heat, stirring, for a few seconds. Remove from the heat and add the milk a little at a time, stirring well between each addition. Return to the heat, then bring to the boil, stirring constantly, and cook until thickened. Remove from the heat, add the nutmeg, mustard and half the cheese and stir well.

◆ Remove the pouch from the water oven, open and gently tip the contents into a large gratin dish. Pour over the cheesy sauce and sprinkle with the remaining cheese.

◆ Place under a preheated grill for 5 minutes, or until golden and bubbling. Serve with a simple salad.

Thai Green Vegetable Curry

500 g (1 lb) squash or pumpkin, peeled, deseeded and cut into chunks

2 red peppers, cored, deseeded and cut into chunks

175 g (6 oz) baby corn, halved

250 g (8 oz) cauliflower florets

2 tablespoons Thai green curry paste

400 g (13 oz) can coconut milk

150 ml (¼ pint) vegetable stock

175 g (6 oz) sugar snap peas

4 tablespoons chopped fresh coriander

Salt and pepper

cooked Thai jasmine rice, to serve

♦ Fill and preheat the water oven to 84°C (183°F).

♦ Place all of the ingredients except the coriander in a large zip seal cooking pouch with a pinch of salt and pepper. Remove as much air as possible using the Archimedes principle (*see page* 7), then seal and submerge for 1½ hours.

♦ Remove the pouch from the water oven and ladle the curry into warmed bowls. Stir in the coriander and serve with Thai jasmine rice.

Serves 4

Hot & Spicy Veggie Jambalaya

2 tablespoons vegetable oil

1 onion, chopped

2 garlic cloves, chopped

200 g (7 oz) long grain rice, rinsed

1 tablespoon Cajun or Creole-style spice mix

1 celery stick, chopped

2 tablespoons tomato purée

2 x 400 g (13 oz) cans chopped tomatoes

1 red and 1 yellow pepper, chopped

1 small courgette, chopped

400 ml (14 fl oz) vegetable stock

Salt and pepper

Chopped flat leaf parsley, to garnish

Hot pepper sauce, to serve (optional)

◆ Fill and preheat the water oven to 84°C (183°F).

◆ Heat the oil in a large frying pan and cook the onions and garlic over a medium heat, stirring frequently, for 8–10 minutes until softened and lightly golden. Add the rice and spice mix with the celery and stir over the heat for 1 minute.

◆ Stir in the tomato purée and the chopped tomatoes, then remove from the heat and transfer to a large zip seal cooking pouch with the remaining vegetables and the stock. Season generously, then remove as much air as possible using the Archimedes principle *(see page 7)*. Seal and submerge for 1 hour 15 minutes until the rice is tender and most of the moisture has been absorbed.

◆ Remove the pouch from the water oven and serve the jambalaya sprinkled with chopped parsley and a few dashes of hot pepper sauce if liked.

Aubergine & Tomato Papardelle with Mozzarella

1 large aubergine, cut into 1.5 cm
(¾ inch) dice

1 onion, chopped

2 garlic cloves, crushed

350 g (11½ oz) homemade or good
quality ready-made tomato pasta sauce

1 teaspoon crushed chilli flakes (optional)

375 g (12 oz) dried pappardelle

250 g (8 oz) buffala mozzarella cheese,
drained and diced

Salt and pepper

To garnish

4 tablespoons grated Parmesan cheese
(optional)

basil leaves, to garnish (optional)

♦ Fill and preheat the water oven to 84°C (183°F).

♦ Place the aubergine in a large zip seal cooking pouch with the onion, garlic, tomato sauce and chilli flakes if using. Season with salt and pepper.

♦ Massage the bag to mix the contents, then remove as much air as possible using the Archimedes principle (*see page* 7). Seal and submerge for 1½ hours.

♦ Meanwhile, cook the pasta according to the packet instructions. Remove from the heat, drain and return to the pan.

♦ Remove the aubergine pouch from the water oven, open and add the aubergines to the pasta with the mozzarella. Toss to mix well, then heap into warmed bowls. Sprinkle over the Parmesan and garnish with basil leaves to serve if liked.

Serves 4

Mixed Bean 'Chilli-sin-Carne'

♦ Fill and preheat the water oven to 84°C (183°F).

♦ Place all of the ingredients except the coriander in a large zip seal cooking pouch and season with salt and pepper. Massage the bag to mix the contents, then remove as much air as possible using the Archimedes principle (*see page* 7). Seal and submerge for 1½ hours.

♦ Remove the pouch from the water oven and ladle into 4 warmed bowls. Top each serving with a tablespoon of soured cream, garnish with chopped coriander and serve with griddled corn tortillas.

1 onion, finely chopped
....
1 celery stick, chopped
....
4 garlic cloves, crushed
....
1 teaspoon crushed chilli flakes
....
2 teaspoons ground cumin
....
1 teaspoon dried oregano
....
1 small cinnamon stick
....
400 g (13 oz) can chopped tomatoes
....
3 x 290 g (9½ oz) canned mixed beans
in spicy sauce
....
Salt and pepper
....
25 g (1 oz) finely chopped fresh coriander,
to garnish
....

To serve
....
4 tablespoons soured cream
....
Griddled corn tortillas
....

Basque-Style Potatoes with Peppers & Preserved Lemon

750 g (1½ lb) baby new potatoes, cut in half
....
1 red onion, halved and thinly sliced
....
2 garlic cloves, chopped
....
1 preserved lemon, finely chopped
....
250 g (8 oz) roasted red peppers, drained and sliced
....
1 teaspoon hot smoked paprika
....
1 teaspoon ground cumin
....
½ teaspoon ground ginger
....
3 tablespoons sun-dried tomato purée
....
1 tablespoon aged sherry vinegar
....
350 ml (12 fl oz) vegetable stock
....
2 tablespoons olive oil
....
Salt and pepper
....
Green salad, to serve (optional)
....

♦ Fill and preheat the water oven to 84°C (183°F).

♦ Place all of the ingredients except the olive oil into a large zip seal cooking pouch. Season with salt and pepper, then massage the bag to mix the contents. Remove as much air as possible using the Archimedes principle (*see page* 7). Seal and submerge for 2 hours.

♦ Remove the pouch from the water oven, open and tip the contents into a large, deep frying pan or shallow roasting dish. Drizzle over the olive oil, then place under a preheated grill for 4–5 minutes until lightly golden and the edges are beginning to crisp.

♦ Serve immediately with green salad if liked.

DESSERTS

Saffron-Poached Figs with Sauternes & Almonds

8 fresh figs, cut in half lengthways

125 ml (4 fl oz) Sauternes dessert wine

2 tablespoons clear honey

Pinch saffron threads

2 tablespoons toasted flaked almonds

Good quality vanilla ice cream, to serve (optional)

♦ Fill and preheat the water oven to 84°C (183°F).

♦ Place the figs in a large zip seal cooking pouch. Mix together the Sauternes, honey and saffron threads in a small jug and pour over the figs. Remove as much air as possible using the Archimedes principle (*see page* 7), then seal and submerge for 30 minutes.

♦ Remove the pouch and transfer the figs to serving dishes, drizzled with the juices. Scatter over the flaked almonds and serve with vanilla ice cream if liked.

Moist Almond Cupcakes with Blackberry Coulis

200 g (7 oz) fresh or frozen blackberries

2 tablespoons freshly squeezed orange juice

50 g (2 oz) vanilla sugar

Almond Cupcakes

125 g (4 oz) butter, softened, plus extra for greasing

125 g (4 oz) caster sugar

1 teaspoon vanilla bean paste or extract

1 teaspoon finely grated lemon rind

75 g (3 oz) ground almonds

2 eggs

2 tablespoons crème fraiche

♦ Fill and preheat the water oven to 84°C (183°F).

♦ Place the blackberries in a large cooking pouch with the orange juice and vanilla sugar and vacuum seal on the gentle / moist setting of the sealer. Submerge for 1 hour.

♦ Meanwhile, grease 8 holes of a cupcake or muffin tin with a little butter.

♦ Beat together all of the ingredients for the cupcakes and divide between the 8 greased holes. Bake in a preheated oven, 180°C (350°F), Gas Mark 4, for 15–18 minutes, or until they are golden and risen and firm to the touch. Remove and cool slightly on a wire rack.

♦ Pour the blackberries from their pouch into a blender or food processor. Blend until smooth, then pour into a jug.

♦ Serve the coulis drizzled over warm almond cupcakes.

Serves 4

Elderflower-Poached Peach Brulée

4 ripe but firm peaches, halved and stoned
....
100 ml (3½ fl oz) water
....
50 ml (2 fl oz) elderflower or pear cordial
....
3 tablespoons clear honey
....
125 g (4 oz) thick Greek yogurt
....
1 teaspoon finely grated orange rind
....
1 tablespoon Cointreau (optional)
....
3 tablespoons soft light brown sugar
....
Crushed amaretti biscuits, to serve
....

♦ Fill and preheat the water oven to 85°C (185°F).

♦ Place the halved peaches in a large zip seal cooking pouch with the water and elderflower cordial along with 2 tablespoons of the honey. Remove as much air as possible using the Archimedes principle (*see page 7*), then seal and submerge for 20 minutes.

♦ Meanwhile, place the Greek yogurt in a bowl with the remaining honey, orange rind and Cointreau if using. Beat together until smooth and thick.

♦ Gently remove the peaches from the pouch, reserving the poaching juices, then arrange cut-side up in a heatproof dish. Sprinkle over the brown sugar and either use a blow torch to lightly caramelize the sugar, or alternatively place under a preheated grill for 1–2 minutes until lightly caramelized.

♦ Arrange the peaches in serving dishes, then top each one with a dollop of yogurt and sprinkle with crushed amaretti biscuits. (For homemade amaretti biscuits, follow the recipe on page 152 but increase the cooking time by a few minutes to take them from soft to crushable). Serve with a small jug of the poaching juices on the side if liked.

Dried Fruit Compote with Homemade Vanilla Ice Cream

250 ml (8 fl oz) milk

6 large egg yolks, lightly beaten

100 g (3½ oz) fine caster sugar

1 teaspoon vanilla bean paste

250 ml (8 fl oz) double cream

Dried Fruit Compote

400 g (13 oz) mixed semi-dried fruit such as apricots, prunes, dates and raisins

350 ml (12 fl oz) freshly squeezed orange juice

3 tablespoons soft brown sugar

1 vanilla pod, split

1 small cinnamon stick

Wafers, to serve (optional)

◆ Fill and preheat the water oven to 85°C (185°F).

◆ In a large bowl, whisk together the milk, egg yolks, sugar and vanilla bean paste. Stir through the cream, then pour into a large zip seal cooking pouch. Remove as much air as possible using the Archimedes principle (*see page* 7). Seal and submerge for 1 hour.

◆ Remove the pouch from the water oven, gently massage the contents until smooth and chill completely in ice cold water. Place in the refrigerator overnight.

◆ Meanwhile, reduce the oven temperature to 70°C (158°F). Place all of the compote ingredients into a large zip seal cooking pouch. Remove as much air as possible using the Archimedes principle. Submerge for about 10 hours, or overnight.

◆ Pour the ice cream custard into the chilled bowl of an ice cream machine and churn according to manufacturer's instructions. Transfer to a chilled container and freeze for 1–2 hours, or until it reaches a scoopable consistency.

◆ Serve the dried fruit compote warm or cold with scoops of vanilla ice cream and wafers on the side if liked.

Serves 4

Gingery Rhubarb Tartlets with Vanilla Cream

500 g (1 lb) rhubarb, trimmed
and cut into chunks
....

50 g (2 oz) caster sugar
....

3 pieces of stem ginger, chopped
....

2 tablespoons stem ginger syrup
....

Pared rind of ½ orange
....

15 g (½ oz) unsalted butter
....

200g (7 oz) sweet shortcrust pastry,
defrosted if frozen
....

plain flour, for dusting
....

1 tablespoon icing sugar, sifted
....

½ teaspoon vanilla extract
....

4 tablespoons crème fraîche
....

♦ Fill and preheat the water oven to 60°C (140°F).

♦ Place the rhubarb in a large cooking pouch with the sugar, chopped ginger, ginger syrup, pared orange and butter. Vacuum seal on the normal / moist setting of the sealer and submerge for 1 hour until the rhubarb is tender.

♦ Meanwhile, roll out the pastry on a lightly floured work surface and use it to line 4 x 10 cm (4 inch) fluted tartlet tins. Prick the base of each a few times with a fork. Line each tartlet case with a piece of scrunched baking parchment and fill with baking beans. Place in a preheated oven, 200°C (400°F), Gas Mark 6, for 15 minutes, then remove the paper and beans and bake for a further 2–3 minutes until crisp and golden.

♦ In a small bowl, stir the icing sugar and vanilla extract into the crème fraîche.

♦ Remove the rhubarb pouch from the water oven and pour the contents into a sieve, reserving the excess juices.

♦ Remove the tartlet cases from their tins. Place each one on a serving plate and fill with the rhubarb mixture. Serve warm with the vanilla cream and a jug of the reserved juices.

Fallen Fruit Crumbles

4 eating apples, peeled, cored and roughly chopped
....
2 teaspoons lemon juice
....
1 teaspoon vanilla bean paste
....
175 g (6 oz) frozen blackberries
....
2 tablespoons soft light brown sugar
....
2 tablespoons caster sugar
....
100 g (3½ oz) plain flour
....
75 g (3 oz) unsalted butter, cut into cubes
....
100 g (3½ oz) porridge oats
....
100 g (3½ oz) demerara sugar
....
½ teaspoon ground cinnamon
....
ice cream, clotted cream or crème fraîche, to serve
....

◆ Fill and preheat the water oven to 84°C (183°F).

◆ Toss the apples in a bowl with the lemon juice and vanilla bean paste, then place in a large cooking pouch with the blackberries, light brown sugar and caster sugar. Vacuum seal on the normal / dry setting of the sealer and submerge for 45 minutes.

◆ Place the flour in a large bowl and use your fingertips to rub the butter into the flour until the mixture resembles coarse breadcrumbs. Stir in the oats, demerara sugar and cinnamon, then spread the mixture out in a baking parchment-lined large roasting tin. Bake in a preheated oven, 200°C (400°F), Gas Mark 6, for 10–15 minutes, stirring occasionally, until crisp and golden.

◆ Remove the fruit from the cooking pouch and spoon into serving bowls. Top with the warm golden crumble and serve with ice cream, clotted cream or crème fraîche.

Serves 4

Boozy Black Forest Brownie Sundaes

250 ml (8 fl oz) milk

6 large egg yolks, lightly beaten

100 g (3½ oz) fine caster sugar

1 teaspoon vanilla bean paste

250 ml (8 fl oz) double cream

450 g (14½ oz) cherries, halved and pitted

4 tablespoons kirsch or cherry brandy

2 large chocolate brownies, broken into pieces

100 ml (3½ fl oz) Belgian chocolate sauce

150 ml (¼ pint) whipping cream, whipped

Coarsely grated chocolate, to decorate

♦ Fill and preheat the water oven to 85°C (185°F).

♦ In a large bowl, whisk together the milk, egg yolks, sugar and vanilla bean paste. Stir through the cream, then pour into a large zip seal cooking pouch. Remove as much air as possible using the Archimedes principle (*see page 7*). Seal and submerge for 1 hour.

♦ Remove the pouch from the water oven, gently massage the contents until smooth and chill completely in ice cold water. Place in the refrigerator overnight.

♦ Pour the ice cream custard into the chilled bowl of an ice cream machine and churn according to manufacturer's instructions. Transfer to a chilled container and freeze for 1–2 hours, or until it reaches a scoopable consistency.

♦ To assemble the sundaes, place a few of the cherries in the base of 4 tall sundae glasses and spoon 1 tablespoon of the kirsch or cherry brandy over the cherries.

♦ Add scoops of ice cream, alternating with pieces of brownie, the remaining cherries and spoonfuls of chocolate sauce. Top with a dollop of whipped cream and a scattering of grated chocolate to decorate.

Rosewater & Cinnamon Apricots with Soft Amaretti Biscuits

500 g (1 lb) apricots, halved and stoned

4 tablespoons clear honey

1 small cinnamon stick

4 cardamom pods, lightly crushed

1 vanilla pod, split lengthways

50 ml (2 fl oz) water

2 tablespoons rosewater

Soft Amaretti Biscuits

1 egg white

75 g (3 oz) ground almonds

50 g (2 oz) caster sugar

Lemon Crème

finely grated rind of 1 lemon

200 ml (7 fl oz) crème fraîche

◆ Fill and preheat the water oven to 84°C (183°F).

◆ Place the apricots in a large zip seal cooking pouch with the honey, cinnamon stick, cardamom pods, vanilla pod, measured water and rosewater. Remove as much air as possible using the Archimedes principle (*see page* 7), then seal and submerge for 30 minutes.

◆ Meanwhile, for the amaretti, whisk the egg white in a grease-free bowl until stiff. Fold in the ground almonds and caster sugar until well mixed. Line a baking sheet with baking parchment and spoon tablespoonfuls of the mixture onto the lined sheet, spaced well apart.

◆ Bake in a preheated oven, 190°C (375°F), Gas Mark 5, for 10 minutes until just beginning to brown. Leave to cool for 5 minutes, then carefully peel away from the paper and transfer to a wire rack.

◆ Make the lemon crème by mixing the lemon rind into the crème fraîche.

◆ Remove the cinnamon stick, cardamom pods and vanilla pod from the apricots and spoon the apricots into serving dishes. Serve with the lemon crème and soft amaretti.

Pancakes with Warm Orange & Blueberry Compote

250 g (8 oz) fresh or frozen blueberries

2 tablespoons freshly squeezed orange juice

1 tablespoon caster sugar

125 g (4 oz) plain flour

1 egg

300 ml (½ pint) milk

50 g (2 oz) butter, melted

Crème fraîche, to serve (optional)

◆ Fill and preheat the water oven to 84°C (183°F).

◆ Place the blueberries in a large cooking pouch with the orange juice and sugar. Vacuum seal on the gentle / moist setting of the sealer, then submerge for 30 minutes.

◆ Meanwhile, sift the flour into a bowl and make a well in the centre. Crack the egg into the well with a splash of milk and begin to blend with an electric hand whisk, slowly adding more milk until the mixture is smooth and all of the milk has been incorporated.

◆ Heat a non-stick pancake pan over a medium–high heat and brush with a little butter. Pour a little pancake mixture into the pan and swirl to coat thinly; the mixture should make 8 pancakes in total. Cook gently for 1–2 minutes, or until pale golden underneath, then flip to cook the other side for a further 30–60 seconds. Transfer to a plate, cover with a piece of baking parchment and repeat the process to make the remaining pancakes.

◆ Remove the cooking pouch from the water oven, open and serve the blueberry compote spooned over the pancakes, with a dollop of crème fraîche if liked.

Serves 4

Rich & Creamy Vanilla Rice Pudding

◆ Fill and preheat the water oven to 83.5°C (182°F).

◆ Mix all of the ingredients together in a large zip seal cooking pouch. Remove as much air as possible using the Archimedes principle (*see page* 7). Seal and submerge for 2½ hours, massaging occasionally until the rice is creamy and tender.

◆ Transfer the rice pudding to an attractive warmed serving dish to serve.

125 g (4 oz) pudding rice

450 ml (¾ pint) milk

50 g (2 oz) caster sugar

1 teaspoon vanilla bean paste or 1 vanilla pod, split

Serves 4–6

Cranberry & Apple Poached Pears

♦ Fill and preheat the water oven to 85°C (185°F).

♦ Place the pears in a large zip seal cooking pouch with the remaining ingredients. Remove as much air as possible using the Archimedes principle (*see page 7*). Seal and submerge for 25 minutes.

♦ Remove and serve the pears warm or cold in serving bowls, ladled with the poaching liquid.

6 large, ripe but firm pears, peeled, cored and quartered
....
600 ml (1 pint) cranberry juice
....
600 ml (1 pint) clear apple juice
....
2–3 tablespoons clear honey, depending on desired sweetness
....
1½ teaspoons vanilla extract
....
2 teaspoons lemon juice
....

Index

Acknowledgments

Photography credits
Octopus Publishing Group Stephen Conroy 72, 89, 94, 95, 97, 109, 113, 125, 128, 131, 143, 146, 148, 153; Will Heap 5, 13, 21, 35, 87, 111, 122, 127, 135, 136, 142, 151; Lis Parsons 1, 3, 14, 17, 27, 28, 33, 52, 57, 67, 69, 70, 73, 74, 77, 79, 81, 82, 84, 93, 98, 108, 114, 117, 121, 133, 137, 141, 155; William Reavell 16, 18, 41, 83, 123, 156; William Shaw 23, 25, 29, 31, 38, 43, 45, 47, 48, 50, 51, 54, 59, 60, 62, 63, 102, 145, 157.

Senior Commissioning Editor: Eleanor Maxfield
Editor: Pollyanna Poulter
Art Direction: Tracy Killick
Designers: Jaz Bahra and Tracy Killick
Photographer: Lis Parsons
Food Stylist: Sue Henderson
Prop Stylist: Liz Hippisley
Production Controller: Sarah Kramer